ICT FOR SOCIAL WELFARE

A toolkit for managers

Luke Geoghegan and Jason Lever
with Ian McGimpsey

The POLICY
PRESS

D0276337

First published in Great Britain in May 2004 by

The Policy Press
University of Bristol
Fourth Floor
Beacon House
Queen's Road
Bristol BS8 1QU
UK

Tel +44 (0)117 331 4054
Fax +44 (0)117 331 4093
e-mail tpp-info@bristol.ac.uk
www.policypress.org.uk

© Luke Geoghegan and Jason Lever 2004

British Library Cataloguing in Publication Data
A catalogue record for this book is available from the British Library.

Library of Congress Cataloging-in-Publication Data
A catalog record for this book has been requested.

ISBN 1 86134 505 4 paperback

Luke Geoghegan is Chief Executive at Toynbee Hall, London and **Jason Lever** is a Senior Policy Officer at the Greater London Authority. **Ian McGimpsey** is Linklaters Volunteer Manager at Toynbee Hall.

The right of Luke Geoghegan and Jason Lever to be identified as authors of this work has been asserted by them in accordance with the 1988 Copyright, Designs and Patents Act.

Cover design by Qube Design Associates, Bristol
Front cover: photograph supplied by www.JohnBirdsall.co.uk
Printed and bound in Great Britain by Latimer Trend and Company Ltd, Plymouth

Contents

List of boxes and figures

Boxes

Figures

Introduction

All too often information and communication technologies (ICT) feel like a problem and not a solution; a cost not an investment; a hindrance not a help in getting the job done. In short, all too often managers and practitioners in social welfare feel crushed by the ICT juggernaut. The aim of this book is to put you back in the driver's seat.

This is not another book about the technicalities of ICT. Indeed, our view is that an overemphasis on the technical aspects of ICT often prevents ICT being used in an effective and creative way. We agree with Frances Cairncross:

> ... what matters most about a new technology is not how it works, but how people use it, and the changes it brings about in human lives. (Cairncross, 2001, p vii)

ICT is often viewed far too narrowly: either seen solely in technical terms or limited to the universal cream-coloured box present on every desk. In this book, ICT is not technical: it is social. Information and communication technologies "are social in that they define how people do things such as how they get information, work, communicate and are educated" (Dutton, 2001, p 4). Indeed, ICT can be defined as "the means by which social interaction is mediated across a series of technological networks" (Fitzpatrick, 2003, p 131). Consequently, ICT can be a powerful tool for social engagement, communication, participation and service delivery. This means that managers and practitioners in social welfare are already in a good position to use ICT effectively; after all, we do have people skills.

This book is aimed at managers and practitioners across social welfare. This includes those working in advice or benefits, those in community development, employment service staff, health practitioners, housing staff, local government officers, rights workers, social care and social work staff, policy analysts, and staff in the voluntary sector as well as community activists and 'social entrepreneurs'. The book will be useful for students and academics in sociology and social policy seeking to link the conceptual themes of their studies with practice and development on the ground.

It is also hoped that, for those of you with the technical understanding of ICT, the unique 'people first' approach used here will prove complementary to your existing skills.

Deployed effectively ICT can improve the services provided by the public and voluntary sectors, empower staff and strengthen the community. ICT also has the capacity to waste a quite extraordinary amount of resources (see Chapter Six), increase staff workloads while decreasing productivity, and further marginalise communities (see Chapter Seven). Therefore, it is in the interests of those working in social welfare to understand and grapple with the issues created by ICT. After all, ICT is far too important to leave to the 'techies'. (However, where specific technical terms are unavoidable we have used them – and provided a glossary.)

There is a wide range of variation in the extent to which ICT is being effectively employed. At one end of the spectrum, voluntary sector organisations with virtually no resources are creating global coalitions for change through ICT (see Chapter Nine). At the other end of the spectrum, major public service providers are denying professional staff access to work-based e-mail facilities (DoH et al, 2002, p 14; DoH, 2003, pp 29-31). This book draws on a wide variety of real-life case studies from a broad range of practice areas (for example, community development, health, housing, crime reduction, social work) that address a number of organisational functions (for example, informing, campaigning, managing), and uses examples that show both good and bad practice. After all, ICT has to work in the real world.

Consequently, at the end of this book the reader should have a good sense of:

- the developing role of ICT in a rapidly changing society and workplace;
- ICT's existing and potential impact on social welfare practice;
- how to improve individual, group and organisational practice through ICT; and,
- developing trends and issues.

In short, the book should provide increased confidence in tackling ICT issues in your workplace.

Chapter One examines ICT in society and explores the implications of this for social welfare practitioners. These ideas, in relation to the values, tools and concepts of social policy, are developed in Chapter Two. Information as a concept in its own right is introduced in Chapter Three, and this lays the foundations for ensuring an understanding of the purpose (rather than merely the process) of ICT. Chapter Four demonstrates how information flows can be modelled and sets out the implications for individuals, teams and organisations. The central concept of content is also explored. These ideas are developed in Chapter Five, where the role of ICT is explored in relation to service and organisational development. Chapter Six unpacks the relationship between an information strategy and ICT strategy, and looks at issues around development, budgeting and implementation. ICT is already creating new forms of social need: so-called information exclusion. Chapter Seven sets out the problems and potential remedies. Chapter Eight looks at government attempts to improve public services through the medium of ICT. Finally, Chapter Nine takes a longer-term look at some of the implications of ICT for social welfare, pointing out some possible implications for democracy, social change and the community.

Naturally, in a book of this length it is impossible to do justice to the full range of issues. But if the material provided here proves to be a useful resource for improving social welfare through the delivery of ICT, then it has served its purpose. To help this process, each chapter concludes with a checklist, or, as we have called it, a 'thinklist'. The questions are framed in such a way that they can be applied to individual practice or team practice, or within the senior management team.

The first step in this process is to begin to thinking of ICT as more than the computer and more than basic software applications (see below). But before exploring the possibilities and problems of these technologies in the world of social welfare practice, we need to take a step back and place ICT firmly in the wider context of people and society.

Defining ICT	
ICT includes	
(but is not restricted to) ...	*... and is used for*
Call centres	Predicting
Computers	Communicating (by text, picture, voice)
Digital cameras	Resourcing (for example, via the Internet)
E-mails	Providing (for example, NHS Direct)
Faxes	Supporting (for example, websites/chat rooms)
Mobile phones	Protecting
Networks	Integrating
PDAs	Managing
Pagers	Recording/monitoring
Photocopiers	Educating and entertaining
Printers	Calculating
Scanners	Consulting
Software	Analysing
Telephones	Campaigning
Websites	Informing

ONE

ICT: people and society

Introduction

The effects of information and communication technology (ICT) are all-pervasive, increasing over time and here to stay. Perhaps less understood are the effects of ICT on social welfare. This chapter provides some important context for social welfare practice by:

• demonstrating the rate of change in relation to ICT;
• introducing some links between ICT and inequality;
• indicating some links between society and ICT;
• summarising the origins of ICT; and
• setting out some key developments associated with the 'information society'.

ICT and the rate of change

Given the statistics on the rate of change, it is not surprising that managers and practitioners feel overwhelmed. Ten years ago the Internet was unheard of outside technical circles. In 2003, 'Half of UK adults (approximately 23 million) currently use the Internet either at home, work, school or various other locations' (www.oftel.gov.uk/publications/research/2003). Some 42% of the population had Internet access at home and 53% of the population had a computer at home. This access was not restricted to the young. Among people aged 35-44, 57% had access to the Internet at home and 71% access to a computer at home. Among 45- to 54-year-olds the figures were 56% and 69% respectively. The time spent connected to the Internet varied between one and two hours (19% of users), three and five hours (20% of users) and six and ten hours (19% of users). Another 28% of users were connected to the Internet in excess of 11 hours per week (www.oftel.gov.uk, 2003).

Apart from the home, the workplace remains the most popular place to access the Internet. Other venues include education establishments (7% of the population), someone else's house (5% of the population), the library (2%) and Internet cafes and kiosks (1%) (www.oftel.gov.uk, 2003).

The spread of the mobile phone has been even quicker and more comprehensive than the Internet: "In 1990 there were just over eleven million mobile telephones worldwide. In 2000 there were 650 million, compared with 500 million personal computers" (Cairncross, 2001, p 41). In the UK,

68% of adults own or use a mobile and 80% of households have at least one mobile (www.oftel.gov.uk, 2002).

In December 2002, sales by the Internet in the UK exceeded £1 billion a month for the first time. Such e-commerce is small in proportion to the overall economy but represents a significant amount of money by anyone's standards (*BBC News*, 2002b).

The impact of ICT on society is indisputable. For the social welfare manager and practitioner, ICT has to be understood in the wider context of, for example, the profound impact on social welfare practice and on how social welfare services are conceived, designed and delivered. The rate of change can often be obscured by conceiving of ICT in the narrowest of terms; for example:

- by regarding ICT simply as personal computers, whereas, as the Introduction showed, ICT covers a wide range of information and communication tools;
- overemphasising the actual technology of ICT at the expense of the purpose or effectiveness of ICT.

Taking a broader perspective is the first step towards using ICT effectively. Furthermore, since these changes are part of the day-to-day environment, the scale of the shift in welfare practice can go unnoticed. A good illustration of this is the telephone. Telephones have been part of everyday life for several generations. But using the telephone to deliver social welfare services was a radical departure (see Box 1.1).

Perhaps the most radical ICT service shift of recent times is NHS Direct. Surely, face-to-face interaction between medical practitioner and patient is essential? Can healthcare really be delivered via phone and Internet? In April 2001 Paul Jenkins of NHS Direct, addressing the conference 'e-Health: a

---

Box 1.1: ICT and radical new forms of social welfare provision

Today telephone helplines are so routine that they escape comment. It was not always the case. In the 1950s, Chad Varah had been alerted to the prevalence of suicide. In *How and why I started the Samaritans*, Chad wrote:

> In an emergency the citizen turns to the telephone and dials 999 ... FIRE it said ... POLICE it said ... AMBULANCE it said.... There ought to be an emergency number for suicidal people, I thought.

By 1953, Chad had telephones and volunteers. On 2 February he called together the volunteers and said: "Over to you Samaritans ... one day everyone will recognise what suicidal people need" (www.samaritans.org.uk). In May 2002 the Samaritans had 4,800,000 contacts; of these, 2,821,000 were verbal (www.samaritans.org.uk). There are 203 centres in the UK and Ireland and there are now telephone helplines for every conceivable need.

---

futurescope', reported that NHS Direct had launched nationally in November 2000. Some five million callers had been provided with assistance. The NHS website (www.nhsdirect.nhs.uk) had launched in December 1999. The end point of contact resulted in 3% of users being referred to the 999 service, 9% going to Accident and Emergency, 30% going to their GP, 21% undertaking routine care and 31% undertaking self-care. Some 95% found the advice they received helpful. Seventy per cent of contacts were out of hours (Jenkins, 2001). While the telephone and website will never replace direct face-to-face contact with medical staff, the system allows people to seek appropriate medical help quickly and effectively and either directed to other forms of healthcare (Accident and Emergency, their GP) or given advice on how to look after themselves, freeing up face-to-face resources for those in acute need.

On 15 April 2003 the Department of Health announced that the service was already dealing with half a million calls per month. Call-handling capacity would be increased from eight million to sixteen million calls by 2006. Additionally, the service would integrate NHS out-of-hours services, reroute 'low priority' 999 calls and establish an NHS Direct digital TV service (DoH, 2003a).

Other examples, which are illustrated more fully elsewhere in this book, include:

- support groups initiated and provided for by websites and chat rooms (Chapter Four);
- new forms of surveillance in the community (Chapter Nine);
- social welfare agencies moving from neighbourhood offices and shifting to telephone call centres (Chapter Six);
- Benefit take-up campaigns through media and interactive websites (Chapter Eight); and
- campaigns for social justice made possible by e-mail and texting (Chapter Nine).

Thomas Kuhn observed the way that groups identified problems and created solutions. Change could be small and incremental. But it could be sudden and sharp – the model shifted so radically and so completely it could not be said to be continuous with what went before; such changes could be described as 'discontinuities'. The model Kuhn developed is instructive for understanding the way society sees and responds to social welfare practice issues; models of work that were commonplace even a few years ago are now frequently rejected (for example, Garret, 2003). Similarly, in social welfare the innovation of today is often commonplace tomorrow. Kuhn (1962) described this process as 'paradigm shift'. Perhaps social welfare, increasingly dependent on ICT, is on the edge of a paradigm shift.

New technology: lessons from history

How society, and consequently social welfare services, respond to new technologies can be explored by examining historical precedents around the introduction of new technologies. Many have argued that society is currently in the middle of another industrial revolution – the information revolution:

> Think of it as one of the three great revolutions in the cost of transport. The nineteenth century, dominated by the steamship and the railway, saw a transformation in the cost of transporting goods; the twentieth century, with first the motor car and then the aeroplane; in the cost of transporting people. The new century will be dominated by the transformation in the cost of transporting knowledge and ideas. (Cairncross, 2001, p 2)

Indeed, it is frequently argued that the different responses by society to new forms of technology (for example, the steam train, the telegraph, the telephone and the TV) are instructive for understanding society's reactions to ICT. In terms of social welfare, Steve Woolgar (1999) has drawn attention to the similar claims between exponents of the telegraph (1840s), radio (1920s), television (1950s) and community video (1970s) and exponents of ICT as a universal panacea for society's ills (see, for example, Standage 1999; Cairncross 2001). Four broad positions often emerge:

* a hope that the new technology will go away;
* profound scepticism towards the new technology;
* unquestioning faith in the new technology; and
* a recognition that under certain circumstances the new technology may be of some use, but only as a means to an end, not an end in itself.

In practice terms this insight is valuable. Staff and their organisations will take a range of views towards ICT. If lack of imagination in seeing the opportunities provided by ICT is one possible problem, excessive belief in the universal efficacy of new technology to solve all the organisation's – indeed society's – ills is another. This phenomenon in the workplace and its management (the four 'I's model) will be examined in Chapter Six. At a national level, the issue of e-government as a means of massively improving service delivery together with ICT as an alleged force for renewing the very foundations of social welfare – democracy – will be dealt with in Chapters Eight and Nine.

ICT and inequality

Questions of poverty, inequality and social exclusion are central to the issues of social welfare practice. Is ICT a neutral force in this process, or has ICT the potential to narrow the gap between rich and poor, as Cairncross (2001) claims? Alternatively, as Castells (2001) argues, is ICT increasing the gap between the haves and the have-nots as well as accelerating the speed with which this is occurring? On the face of it, the omens do not look good. There is a strong correlation between social class and ICT use. A common categorisation of social class is that of a spectrum from A to E, in which categories A and B represent the professional and managerial classes, and D and E represent unskilled manual workers. The 1998 'IT for All' survey 'showed that only 30% of DEs had used a computer as opposed to 74% of ABs and only 6% of DEs had access to the Internet at home as opposed to 27% of ABs' (IT for All, 2000). This 'digital divide' and practical ways of bridging it are explored in Chapter Seven.

The relationship between gender and ICT is complex (see, for example, Dutton, 2001; Webster, 2001a, 2001b). However, the Department for Education and Employment, drawing on its research 'IT for All', reports (DfEE, 2000, p 46):

- Women have lower rates of computer and Internet usage than men – only 51% of female respondents in 1998 had used a computer, as opposed to 65% of male respondents; 22% of female respondents had used the Internet as opposed to 35% of male respondents.
- Women are less likely to have access to a computer at home (39% as opposed to 49% of men) or at work (44% as opposed to 55% of men).
- Women rated their computer skills lower than men did.
- Women were less likely to see the Internet as being useful to them – only one third of women thought it would be as opposed to half the male sample.

Gender is thus an important factor with implications for the design, delivery, training and uptake of ICT in the organisation (see Chapter Seven).

The Internet is frequently promoted as a great resource accessible to all. Perhaps it is – for those whose first language is English (see Box 1.2).

Box 1.2: The language of the web

English is now the dominant or official language in over 60 countries ... [it] is primarily the result of two factors: the expansion of British colonial power, which peaked towards the end of the 19th century, and the emergence of the United States as the leading economic power of the 20th century. (Crystal, 1997, pp 106, 107)

It is now also the dominant language of the web: "In 1999 78.3% of all websites world-wide were in English" (OECD, cited by Cairncross, 2001, p 281). The biggest producer of intellectual property (for example, software, drugs, films, and music) is the US; the second biggest is the UK. Almost all the scientific material on the website is in English (Cairncross, 2001, p 281). What does this say about the future of multiculturalism and diversity?

ICT and sociology

Margaret Thatcher proclaimed that "there is no such thing as society". The reality is rather different. The discipline of sociology born at the beginning of one industrial revolution and providing the analytic and conceptual tools for understanding welfare practice is highly relevant to understanding the current situation and relating its impact to social welfare. As Giddens puts it: "Sociology is a social science, having as its main focus the study of the social institutions brought into being by the industrial transformations of the past two or three centuries" (Giddens, 2001, p 5). Consequently, sociology provides some essential starting points for those in practice to think about ICT and its implications:

- community;
- communication and the mass media;
- gender and age;
- education;
- politics, power dissent and control; and
- culture, particularly the culture of the workplace.

Community

Communities are often seen as being linked to geographical space – a particular physical location. However, what are described as 'communities of interest' – that is, people drawn together across 'space and place' by commonalities – have always existed parallel to geographical communities. ICT has increased the range and intensity of these communities of interest. Networking can be defined as "the process by which relationships and contacts between people or organisations are established, nurtured and utilised for mutual benefit" (Gilchrist, 2000, p 2). Increasingly, however, networking is synonymous with the linking together of ICT equipment and the process of group communication via this technology. As Wellman puts it: "When computer networks link people as well as machines, they become social networks'" (Wellman and Haythornthwaite, 2002, p 326).

Thus, a hundred years ago people meeting up to discuss a particular interest were often the well-to-do. Now, via telephone and Internet, people can share a range of minority interests (including varieties of pornography) with ease. Similarly, people who suffer from similar problems increasingly 'meet' online to share resources and support (see Chapter Five). ICT has also enabled campaigns for social justice (see Chapter Nine), allowed immigrant groups to access news and culture from the mother country and allowed people to develop knowledge and skills. These so-called virtual communities have often developed independently of any formal 'social welfare' input (see, for example, Pleace et al, 2003).

Issues of 'space and place' also apply to the work of practitioners. Thus, for the social welfare practitioner and manager, ICT is increasing the ability to work from home, mediated by fax, e-mail and the Internet (so-called teleworking). Is allowing flexible work without the chore of commuting an advantage or a way in which work further invades the home (see, for example, Dutton, 2001)? The possibilities of distance learning for the social welfare professional have now evolved into e-learning, whereby students can draw materials from the web, talk with students online and attend virtual lectures.

Issues of space and place are closely linked with inequality. Sociologists have long been interested in the differences and similarities between urban and rural communities. For ICT optimists, the new technologies will allow *all* cities to access opportunity and wealth (Cairncross, 2001); for others, ICT merely accelerates the growing divide between cities of the Third and First Worlds and, in England, between London and the provincial cities and between town and country – see Chapter Seven (Castells, 2001).

Communications and mass media

ICT is profoundly shaping communications that are one-to-one, within the group and within society as a whole (the mass media). At the one-to-one level, much of our communication is supported by face-to-face contact. Even on the telephone, non-verbal skills help us assess the meaning of what is being said to us – for example, via the tone of voice. New forms of electronic communication mean that these non-verbal and context-specific cues are often absent.

The French philosopher Jean Baudrillard coined the term 'simulacrum': the collapse of the difference between image and reality. ICT, through ever more advanced technology, convinces us that what we see and hear is in fact reality – what Baudrillard (1988, 2000) calls 'hyper-reality' (see also Horrocks and Jevtic, 1999). The problem is that this collapse between image and reality and the creation of false images of physical perfection can lead to problems for those who have disabilities, such as non-standard bodies, or those with image disorders, such as anorexia. Image manipulation can also degrade (for example, synthesised pornographic images of women and children).

Gender and age

ICT use is often portrayed by the media as the preserve of males. The male can be glamorous (the up-and-coming business leader frequently depicted in the advertisements) or a 'nerd'. In the mainstream media this male is predominantly white. There is a tradition in which technology is seen as the preserve of the male (Webster, 2001a, 2001b, Harlow, 2003, pp 16–18). A quick perusal of the computer and video games on sale shows that the vast majority of them conform to the worst stereotypes of the male market.

The *perception* of ICT, then, as a male preserve may well put off workforces in the social welfare fields, the majority of whose staff are often female – for example, nursing, social work and primary school teaching. In a similar vein,

ICT is almost always portrayed as the preserve of the young. Where older people are portrayed with ICT, the message (whether implicit or explicit) is often that this is amazing and worthy of comment. Again, such perceptions will be reflected in the workplace. Managers and practitioners may not be in a position to change these media stereotypes, but they certainly need to be aware that they are prevalent and may well affect the workplace.

Education

What people are taught, what information they are provided with, by society generally and within particular cultures, is of great interest to the sociologist. For what is learned is highly influential in our collective views about what is and is not acceptable in culture and society. The learning process can be narrowly defined (the school curriculum) or more broadly defined (work or professional culture), or the 'lessons' drawn from the mass media (see, for example, Giddens, 2002, for a good overview).

In the school curriculum, a chicken-and-egg situation has developed: ICT has become part of the curriculum because of the importance of ICT in society, which almost guarantees that the relative importance of ICT in succeeding generations will continue to grow, thus further influencing the curriculum, and so on (see, for example, DfEE, 1997). Indeed, the *Independent on Sunday* (Hirst, 2003) reported that 99% of schools now have access to the Internet compared with 28% in 1998. It continued: "Recent studies have shown that children perform better through key stages 2, 3 and 4 of the National Curriculum when computers are used as part of the teaching". That is to say, children not only learn *about* ICT but learn *through* ICT. Again, this has implications for the practitioner. It is noticeable how younger staff – of whatever level – in an organisation are often the most comfortable with ICT. This often translates into a willingness and ability to access information (for example, via the Internet) before it occurs to older staff to do the same.

Politics, power, dissent and control

An abiding concern of sociology is the exercise of power. In the late 1980s and early 1990s technology brought these issues to the fore with the increasing installation of close circuit television (CCTV) and the introduction of electronic tagging. The debate was between those who claimed these innovations would protect 'law-abiding citizens' who, naturally, had nothing to fear from these technological innovations and those who feared an invasion of privacy and greater state control (see, for example, Ericson and Haggerty, 2001). The possibilities of ICT have raised the stakes considerably in this debate through the possibility of greater monitoring and control of individuals both in the workplace (see, for example, Huntington and Sapey, 2003) and in society at large through, for example, ID cards and facial recognition software. This will be explored in more detail in Chapter Nine.

At the same time ICT has considerable potential to help deviant groups organise on a scale that would have been inconceivable even a few years ago. Paedophile Internet groups, extremist political groups and organised crime have all made good use of ICT. But how is a balance achieved between the rights of the individual and the rights of the community? A good example of how ICT brings these issues sharply in focus is the question of whether the community has the right to know whether a convicted paedophile is living in the neighbourhood (see Box 1.3).

Box 1.3: Is a paedophile living in my neighbourhood?

In the US, residents of the state of Minnesota have the option of finding out whether a convicted paedophile or sex offender is living in the neighbourhood. The twin cities of St Paul and Minneapolis make up the major conurbation in Minnesota. Visit the website of St Paul Police, www.ci.stpauls.mn.us/depts/police and click on 'Sex Offender Notification' (accessed 3 December 2003).

In fact, research shows that there is no evidence that such community notification improves the protection of children (Lovell, 2001). Indeed, such notification might even encourage law breaking by vigilante groups.

Culture

For the sociologist, culture is not just national culture mediated by language, religion and ethnicity, or the highbrow arts such as opera. It is:

> ... those aspects of human societies which are learned, rather than inherited. These elements of culture are shared by members of society and allow cooperation and communication to take place. They form the common context in which individuals in a society live their lives. A society's culture comprises both intangible aspects – the beliefs, ideas, and values which form the content of culture – and tangible aspects – the objects, symbols or technology which represents that content. (Giddens, 2001, p 23)

So cultures are not just constructed around ethnicity, language and religion. There are also cultures of the workplace (see, for example, Wilson and Rosenfield, 1990; Handy, 1993); what has been described as 'the way we do things around here' (a phrase deriving from an internal ICL publication: *The ICL way: The way we do things around here*, cited by Wilson and Rosenfield, 1990, p 229). Handy (1993, p 180) puts it like this:

> So too, anyone who has spent time with any variety of organisations, or worked in more than two or three, will have been struck by the differing atmospheres, the different ways of doing things, the differing levels of energy,

> of individual freedom, of kinds of personality.... They have differing cultures
> – sets of values and norms and beliefs – reflected in different structures and
> systems.

This is not simply an academic nicety. Since the work culture of (say) the Royal Marines, an art college and a local government office are different, individuals moving from one culture to another will have to make accommodations or may find the experience difficult, possibly even painful. This is the point where culture intersects with power. Handy again: "In organisations there are deep-set beliefs about the way work should be organised, the way authority should be exercised, people rewarded, people controlled ... what combination of obedience and initiative is looked for in subordinates?" (Handy, 1993, p 181).

Managers and practitioners dealing with ICT in the workplace need to recognise the prevailing cultural mindset. As has already been shown, this may be influenced by the composition of the staff in terms of gender, social class and age. Staff may see the introduction of ICT systems as an attempt to change work for the worse, disempowering them and marginalising their existing work. They may be right.

Additionally, several cultures can coexist in the same workplace. The culture of a surgical team is different from the culture of hospital social workers, even though ostensibly both are working in a hospital and both are working in the welfare field of 'health and social care'. And different workplace groups – sometimes in close proximity – can have very different perspectives on the efficacy of ICT.

Views about ICT can also be shaped by the collective professional view. Many professions and workers distinguish their working culture quite clearly from those outside the group (for example, Giddens, 2001, p 294). In their attempt to differentiate themselves from lay persons, all professions and many work cultures almost routinely express the view that 'they' (that is, the 'outsiders', non-professionals) fail to understand the (invariably) complex issues that the professional is wrestling with and that as a result intervention from these 'outsiders', whether inspection agencies (such as the Audit Commission or Ofsted), elected members of government (whether local or national), or service users, is often inappropriate. If 'outsider' groups argue for a greater deployment of ICT, this can become a friction point. Further, the wider debate of whether ICT is a force for good – or bad – is reflected in the culture of the workplace. Thus, some see ICT as inherently controlling (for example, Henman and Adler, 2003; Huntington and Sapey, 2003) and some as a weapon of liberation (for example, Parry, 2001; *The Economist*, 2003).

If the notion of workplace cultures – and the wider influences upon them – is accepted, it makes sense to understand the professional culture before recommending, establishing or changing ICT systems. The interface between work culture and ICT and its implications are tackled in more detail in Chapter Six.

Of course, ICT workers have their own culture too. The specific use of language ('jargon') is a good way of differentiating the profession or workplace culture from 'outsiders'. Brown and Duguid (2002) provide a comprehensive debunking of this kind of terminology. For those involved in the technical side of ICT, it is essential continually to put people and straightforward communication at the heart of design, development and delivery of ICT.

Finally, it is worth pointing out that these forces cannot be studied at arm's length. After all, we are all part of society and thus cannot distance ourselves from it. Similarly with ICT and society: since we are part of society, we are all, to a greater or lesser extent, users of ICT, whether directly (through our PC) or indirectly (many of the services we receive could not be delivered without ICT). So part of the process of thinking about ICT in relation to our work is reflecting on our own attitudes to technology and specifically ICT. What is required is what C. Wright Mills (1970) called the 'sociological imagination', an attempt to get out of one's existing mindset and to try to understand the mindset of someone else. It is here that the social welfare practitioner has an unparalleled advantage. A lifetime of empathising with others helps the practitioner to imagine the perspective of others. This is invaluable in using and developing ICT in a creative and responsible manner.

ICT: origins and implications

Finally, understanding the origins of ICT is helpful to understanding its current form. Like many other technological innovations, many of the elements of ICT sprang from military needs. Indeed, the first computer (Colossus) was developed at Bletchley Park as a means of deciphering enemy codes during the Second World War (www.bletchleypark.co.uk). Later, the Internet came about as a result of a desire to harness the scarce resource of existing computers in a joint endeavour, and was funded by the American Defense Department's Advanced Research Projects Agency (ARPA); the connections established were known as ARPANET. To ensure that the system could survive a military attack, a model was developed whereby information could travel by a variety of routes to the same destination; thus, if one node of the network was knocked out, the overall network could still function:

> In 1974 TCP/IP (Transmission Control Protocol/Internet Protocol) which lays down the format in which all data sent over the Internet is packaged, was designed.... It was introduced formally in 1983, the date usually taken as the Internet's proper starting point. (Cairncross, 2001, p 34)

The use of computers became more widespread and by 1990 the concept of hypertext was developed by Tim Berners-Lee. Hypertext is a mechanism for cross-referencing material between different computers. In 1991 Berners-Lee developed a program called a 'browser' that allowed computer users to view material stored on other computers. Thus, 1991 is generally regarded as the birthday of the World Wide Web (Cairncross, 2001; Castells, 2001).

According to Castells, the Internet has a specific culture, a curious product of what he calls the 'hacker ethic' and capitalism. Castells's view of the hacker culture is both subtle and complex. In his lexicon hackers are not "reckless computer geeks aiming to crack codes, illegally penetrate systems, or bring havoc to computer traffic". Rather, Castells (2001, p 41) quotes Raymond: "… a shared culture of expert programmers and networking wizards that traces its history back through decades" (see also Jordan and Taylor, 2001; Kirkpatrick, 2002).

The hacker tradition lives on both as a positive force – for example, in Linux and the open source movement (see Chapter Nine) – and as a negative force through those who create computer viruses. However, the reality is that much of the commercially available conception, design, production and distribution of ICT equipment is firmly in the realm of the private sector. This gives rise to six phenomena:

- *Duplication:* different companies will develop different products to meet similar needs. For example, in the 1980s there were several major models of computer operating systems. The contemporary equivalent might be rival systems for wireless networks.
- *Proliferation:* in a period of technological innovation there will be no shortage of new ICT products on the market. A very large proportion of these will fail or will add little value for their comparatively high price or will be outdated so rapidly as to make purchase not worthwhile.
- *Incorrect and uncertain predictions:* incorrect forecasts about the future role of a new technology are widespread. For example, many miscalculated the value of dot.com companies. On many products the jury is still out. Third Generation (G3) mobile phone technology is perhaps the most recent example. In April 2000, four telephone companies spent some £22.5 billion in an auction to acquire the rights to enhanced bandwidth. However, at the time of writing only one of these companies – the company '3' – has actually brought a product to market that can make use of this technology (Islam, 2003).
- *Protection:* companies need to recoup their investments. Digital technology means that perfect copies of products (such as software, CDs, DVDs) can be made quickly and virtually free. This benefits the company profit sheet. It also makes the risk of piracy a problem of major proportions and explains why ICT companies attach such importance to protecting their intellectual property rights.
- *Standardisation:* the diversification of products is quickly followed by the need to standardise products. From the consumer's point of view, standardisation is necessary to allow different ICT systems to work together. Producers, for their part, are tempted to ensure that the standard that evolves

is the one that only they have intellectual property rights to – thus eliminating commercial competition.

- *Coping with a finite market:* the market for ICT is relatively finite. From a company perspective, consumers who buy an upgrade every two or three years are preferable to those who rest content with their product for the next 10 or 20 years. The ICT market is, of course, not unique in this respect. Perhaps the ICT market is unique, however, around the operation of the so-called Moore's Law, which is often stated thus: the cost of computing power halves every 18 months. (This 'law' is in wide circulation; this version is from Mulgan, 1998, p 31.) Certainly, ICT appliances seem to fall in price in both real and relative terms while increasing in capability and decreasing in physical size.

These factors all contribute to a culture of, in the words of Heeks (1999, p 34), "this year's IT can solve ... problems better than last year's". For the practitioner, these phenomena have a profound effect on those involved in the purchase and management of ICT systems and those using them (see Box 1.4).

Some practical aids for navigating these hazards are set out in Chapter Six.

Box 1.4: Purchasing hazards

- Purchasing can be a hazardous business given that the market is awash with products; the situation is continually changing and none of the products has a long pedigree.
- The newest products need not necessarily be the best or meet a need that actually exists.
- Failure to manage the products effectively – for example, pirated software on office machines – can lead to severe penalties.
- Balancing the risk of 'standard' but perhaps sub-optimal products with optimal products that may be subsequently forced out of the market.
- Rapid turnover of products meaning that even the most cutting-edge product is near obsolescence in three years' time.

Source: Heeks (1999, p 34)

ICT, people and society: some emerging trends

This interplay of technological, commercial and societal forces around ICT is usually credited with giving rise to a number of trends:

The rise of the knowledge worker and the knowledge economy: according to this notion, production has shifted from predominantly tangible goods (coal, steel, ships, cars) to less tangible goods and services. Unlike with previous generations, manual production has been demoted, to be replaced by brainwork; the gathering, managing, storing, retrieving and transmission of knowledge before applying this knowledge to particular situations. To parallel the knowledge worker, there is also a knowledge or information economy: "an economic system dominated by industries that produce, manipulate and/or transmit information, more narrowly that sector of the economy constituted by such industries" (Sassen, 2000, p 178; see also Giddens, 2001, p 294.)

Education and entertainment – and their hybrid, 'infotainment' – are major components of the knowledge economy (for example, Leadbeater, 2000). Such an economy generates real wealth. In April 2003 the media gave wide coverage to the fact that the wealth of the creator of Harry Potter – J.K. Rowling – had surpassed the wealth of the Queen of England. This was despite the Queen's legacies from many generations, her land, property, income and other assets. Infotainment is perhaps not new: Dickens created fiction that raised issues about profound social problems. What is perhaps new is the way that infotainment is now a frequent feature of social welfare; thus, a storyline that had been planted in Independent Television's *Coronation Street* about encouraging people to use ICT took up a concurrent government campaign theme (*The Guardian*, 2003).

However, many versions of this argument understate just how long 'knowledge workers' have existed. If it is agreed that bankers and lawyers should be classified as knowledge workers, then knowledge workers were very much a feature of medieval Europe. Certainly, early social workers and housing workers under Octavia Hill in Victorian England look remarkably like knowledge workers too (Whelan, 2001). Nevertheless, it seems fair to say that knowledge workers as a proportion of the total labour force have increased, that ICT has helped knowledge workers in their tasks, and that virtually all of those in social welfare would qualify as knowledge workers under this broad definition (see, for example, Webb, 2003, p 235).

Where the concept of the knowledge worker and the knowledge economy is helpful from a practice point of view is in highlighting that gathering, managing, storing, retrieving and transmitting information is a continuous and dynamic process that is central to social welfare practice (see Chapter Three).

The collapse of distance/time constraints: this observation rests on the assumption that the costs of communication have fallen in real and comparative terms. This is reflected in the costs of, say, transatlantic phone calls and international flights. Further technological advances have meant that websites anywhere in the world can be visited from a computer in the UK for the price of a local telephone call and that groups can communicate internationally via e-mail and chat rooms both in 'real time' and 'asynchronously' (that is, the process whereby information can be stored and reaccessed at any time through, for example, e-mail, voice mail, or video).

In turn, this has given rise to the concept of the '24/7 society', that is, a society in which activities can take place 24 hours a day, seven days a week (see, for example, Leadbeater, 2000). For a commercial firm this has advantages; there can be a continuous cycle of work (without anyone having to work the night shift) by sending certain types of work-in-progress backwards and forwards across time zones. What is frequently forgotten is that many social welfare services have been 24/7 from their inception (for example, health practitioners). These potential and pitfalls of increasing social welfare service availability are explored in more detail in Chapter Eight.

The faster, faster society: this is a corollary of the collapse of distance/time constraints. Where no boundaries are observed – in terms of either time or geography – there is an inevitable consequence that needs and desires are expected to be resolved quicker, possibly even instantaneously (see C. Leadbeater, 2000; Eriksen, 2003). At a personal level this can give rise to stress, lack of motivation and/or resistance in relation to ICT in the workplace and to the phenomenon of 'information overload' – issues and solutions that will be explored in successive chapters.

Extended to social welfare policy, this may foster the view that long-term social problems can be solved instantaneously by yet more new legislation, capacity building in the voluntary sector can occur overnight, 'healthy living' can be achieved over only slightly longer periods and 'neighbourhood renewal' can turn around in a couple of years areas that have been in decline for generations (Knutt, 2003).

Globalisation: the term 'globalisation' occurs almost invariably with ICT. Globalisation can be defined as: "The growing interdependence between different peoples, regions and countries in the world as social and economic relationships come to stretch world wide" (Giddens, 2001, p 690).

Certainly, ICT has helped the process of globalisation. What is less clear is the extent to which globalisation is a force in shaping social welfare practice. It could be argued that globalisation generates social need (via economic migration, for example, or the underground drugs economy) and that social welfare practice is increasingly influenced by social welfare policy and practice in other countries. But both these issues are beyond the scope of this book.

Changing patterns of work: ICT is often credited with a 'disintermediating' effect. This argument is based on the view that the size and complexity of society needs multiple intermediaries: in the private sector between the purchaser and the provider (such as insurance brokers, travel agencies); politically (for example, representative politicians); educationally (teachers and librarians); and in the workplace (middle management). These intermediaries add 'transaction costs', the cost of having a third party involved. In contrast, ICT has the potential to dissolve this 'transactional glue': thus, the airline ticket can be bought directly from the household PC rather than a travel agent (Evans and Wurster, 2000), politically an electronic vote can be cast direct (Adonis and Mulgan, 1997), educationally there is 'distance learning' (Brown and Duguid, 2002), and the organisation can be 'delayered' of middle management and consequently organisational processes rethought (Hammer, 1990).

This can go so far as to create a 'virtual' organisation: "the organisation exists, but you can't see it. It is a network not an office" (Handy, 1996, p 114). The reality is rather different. For example, research has shown that organisations have not become flatter (Brown and Duguid, 2002, p 28). Perhaps it is nearer the truth to say that ICT changes the position and function of intermediaries rather than abolishes them altogether.

Put baldly, the changes related to ICT can seem overwhelming. However, the reality is that at heart these technologies remain social. New technologies such as the telephone, radio and telephone have been adopted in the home and workplace without too much long-term difficulty. The revolution of yesterday becomes the commonplace of today (Wellman and Haythornthwaite, 2002).

Thinklist

- **What resources (time, energy, money) do you invest in ICT?**
- **Has this gone up, down, or stayed the same over the past five years?**
- **What has been positive about this? What has been negative?**

TWO

ICT and social welfare practice

Introduction

In Chapter One, key concepts in ICT were defined and its growth across society was explored in a number of welfare, leisure and commercial settings. In this chapter, the focus is on introducing the key issues and applications of ICT to the social welfare professional and practitioner. The essential context for the delivery of – and citizen experience of – social welfare services will be provided in a broad outline of seven major concepts of social policy and an introduction to their relationship with ICT.

The concepts of *social rights* and *citizenship*, and their interrelationship, will be examined first. This will lead to a discussion of how *social needs* can be met, in particular moving on to the principles of addressing *access to services by marginalised groups*. The contribution of *advocacy* and *self-help* will be introduced here. This will provide a basis for exploring several dimensions of community and capitalism – the thesis of *commodification* and how it underpins notions of consumerism, citizenship and empowerment. Finally, we shall look at the role of *community development* and the current emphasis on the cultivation of *social capital*.

Subsequent chapters will refer to these core social policy concepts. Indeed, a central, recurring theme will be that ICT is irrevocably part of the social welfare equation. ICT both helps professionals to work within and across their disciplines and agency boundaries and can directly enhance citizens' accessibility, convenience and needs satisfaction in receiving social welfare services. This central thesis will be analysed at 'micro' levels of professional and organisational practices in Chapters Four to Seven, at a 'macro' level of e-government policies in Chapter Eight, and through the individual as 'citizen' versus 'consumer' debate, which we return to in Chapter Nine.

The second part of the chapter will consider central aspects of the safeguards for ensuring confidentiality of data and privacy of information. This will include the importance of Internet safety for a particularly vulnerable group of users: children and young people.

Key concepts of social policy

Social rights

It was only in the modern period that (*social*) rights came to be seen as "rights to resources (to welfare, health, education, income and social security)". Previously, rights were conceptualised as *civil* (freedom from coercion) and *political* (right to vote), and relief from poverty or ill-health was not conceived in terms of rights and citizenship (Plant, 1992, p 15).

While civil and political rights relate to a set of negative liberties ('freedom from'), social rights relate to the ability to do certain things for which health, education and income are necessary ('freedom to'). Therefore, in theory, social rights are infinite, as there are no clear limits to these services. This fundamental issue is developed later in the section on meeting social needs, since a concept of need underlies such positive rights.

A distinction needs to be made between *substantive* and *procedural* rights. The former are "rights to a good or service which is claimed", although in practice their application is limited by the application of professional discretion or political prioritisation. The latter include "rights to information, and to rights which make the redress of grievances possible" (Spicker, 1995, p 172). Procedural rights can be regarded as a tool for the service user to self-address his or her "low status, experience … [of] discrimination" by helping to see himself or herself as "the owner and potential enforcer of rights" (Harris, 1999, p 931). This is now expressed as user or citizen empowerment.

Citizenship

In the classic 1950s formulation of T.H. Marshall, citizenship confers "a [social] right to a central set of resources which can provide economic security, health and education". In linking the "rights to welfare" with the idea of social justice, the capitalist view was challenged that "a person's status in economic and social terms is to be determined [only] by the market" (Plant, 1992, p 16). The contemporary focus is on how citizenship is supposed to confer an "equal status on all citizens, regardless of sex, race, ethnicity, or religion" as well as regardless of income (Phillips, 2000, p 37). In terms of the social policy implications of Marshall's values, the milestone report of the Seebohm Committee (1968) sought to reshape post-war social services in the UK on the basis of a "commitment to citizenship rights, enshrined in universal services". Accordingly, "families with a variety of problems in whatever social circumstances" would benefit from support (Harris, 1999, p 919; Malin et al, 2002, p 54).

There has been a gradual shift over the past two to three decades from promoting 'good citizenship' – and the values of obeying the law and social customs – towards "active citizenship" (Crick, 2000, p 78). However, the New Right challenge in the 1980s saw a reappraisal of the concept to ascribe the "active citizens' label to those able to stand alone, independent in the market ... [and free] from the dependency culture and the welfare state" (Lister, 1990, cited in Harris, 1999, p 922). Since the late 1990s, however, the need to promote 'active citizenship' has been linked by New Labour with attempts to tackle social exclusion through developing *social capital*.

While current UK government policy still has a focus on 'good citizenship' – enforced, for example, through a punitive approach to antisocial behaviour and youth crime – a key milestone in its view of citizenship was the incorporation of aspects of citizenship in the National Curriculum in England in 2002. In turn, this recognised that the impact of citizenship education through schools and voluntary activities was not sufficient and would be limited by scarce social capital in the communities that children live because of, for example, poverty and high mobility. Indeed, this approach argues that the rights (and responsibilities) of citizenship are learned through 'civil society' – that is, the family, trade union, congregation, or voluntary institutions within a neighbourhood (Alexander, 2003, p 26). This is explored in the following sections on 'meeting social needs' and 'community development and social capital'.

The argument that access to ICT should be seen as an essential component of the rights of citizenship will developed in Chapter Eight.

Meeting social needs

At its simplest, "meeting needs is what public services ought to be about" (Percy-Smith, 1996, p 3). The central role of needs in relation to rights and citizenship within a universal welfare system has been set out by Raymond Plant. If there are such things as basic needs, then these should be used "to underpin a set of enforceable social rights". Inequalities, arising from the operations of markets, should not just be accepted, since "citizenship confers a right to a central set of resources which can provide economic security, health and education" (Plant, 1991, 1992, cited in Percy-Smith, 1996, p 7; Sanderson, 1996, p 25).

The New Right's critique is that the definition of needs will be for ever expanded under the pressure of interest groups, including those of social welfare professionals and bureaucrats (Plant, 1992, p 18). Hence, a market-based society, which maximises the scope of individual choice and relegates the state to a minimal 'safety net' role, is the preferred basis for welfare provision (Sanderson, 1996, p 11).

The contested view of the social needs for resources to exercise rights links closely with the concept of poverty. More specifically, it relates to whether poverty is conceived in absolute terms – as "a condition under which people are unable to obtain subsistence, or the basic necessities of life", in Peter Townsend's formulation (Townsend, 1980, p 299). Alternatively, proponents of a concept of relative poverty point to the problematic nature of such a 'poverty line', in that numbers below that line may decrease yet the 'poverty gap' between different groups may still increase. (For further analysis, see Townsend, 1979; Sen, 1985; Ringen, 1988.)

In the post-war period, within UK social welfare services, "the rational administration of bureaucratic systems and professional expertise in control over the content of services" were combined. With priority assigned to the 'expert knowledge' of professionals, and citizen passivity assumed, the predominant social welfare model "allowed professionals to be unaccountable to users of the services they provided" (Harris, 1999, p 918). However, over the past two decades, it has been argued that 'deprofessionalisation' led to a change in the professional–client relationship (Elston, 1991, cited in Surender and Fitzpatrick, 1999, p 500). In essence, this suggests that there is a shift in power relationships between the social welfare professional and the citizen user, based on a reduction of the former's authority and an enhancement of the latter's understanding of the issues affecting them. By increasing the level of, and ready access to, information available to the citizen, ICT can act as a driver of this process. For example, in the field of medicine, with a global online market for health information, "patients may find it increasingly difficult to accept the non-availability of a drug in the UK if they have access to information proving efficacy in other countries" (Kendall, 2000, p 21).

A further, contributing factor to changing models of meeting social needs may be 'proletarianisation'. This describes "the process by which an occupational category is divested of control over certain prerogatives" (Surender and Fitzpatrick, 1999). For example, in personal social services, growing proceduralisation and senior workers or managers acting as "gatekeepers to resources" can lead to front-line social workers having "the role of gathering information for assessment, but on the periphery of the formal decision-making process" (Watson, 2002, p 883).

These theories of meeting social needs underpin and support the range of social welfare services provided across the range of agencies.

Improving access to services by marginalised groups

There is a key relationship between problems in access to services by marginalised groups and social capital. The concept of 'network poverty', to quote Pierson, describes the weakness in social networks experienced by groups, families and individuals. It is these "social supports and informal help" that are part of participation at community level and that enable enjoyment of "the standards of living shared by the majority of people" (Pierson, 2002, p 12). Social capital is therefore built up through "close, supportive networks embedded in everyday relationships of friends, neighbourhood and family", which, in turn, provide "crucial information for individuals and families on jobs, education, training and a range of options for advancing individual interests" (Pierson, 2002, p 13).

This theme will be developed further in the later section, 'community development and social capital'. Traditionally, ICT is seen as an outside irrelevance, yet the potential – and current limitations – of ICT in enhancing access to social welfare services by marginalised, or socially excluded, groups will be outlined in discussion of the 'digital divide' in Chapter Seven.

Commodification: consumerism, citizenship and empowerment

As stated earlier, the opportunity for citizens to exercise choice in the operation of UK social welfare services has often been limited (Spicker, 1995, p 160). The seeds of the emergence of a consumerist model of public services provision can be seen in 'clientism'. In the UK, this describes the post-war relationship of welfare services to their users, who were "seen as recipients of services planned for them" (Hudson, 1998, p 456).

What is characterised as the 'commodification' effect relates to different conceptions of *citizen*. The primary conception is a 'consumer model', according to which citizens are entitled to expect a certain standard of service or provision, and are empowered to seek compensation or redress if the service is not satisfactory (D. Miller, 2000, p 28). In the 1980s and 1990s, 'welfare pluralism' was developed as the idea of empowering citizens with individual choice – to transform them into 'consumers' – and lay at the centre of UK government policies of introducing quasi-markets into health and other welfare services. ('Quasi-markets' was a term used to describe the limited choices available to patients under the purchaser–provider split existing in general practitioner fund-holder practices; Malin et al, 2002, p 55.)

The main principle is that decisions should be made by the person receiving the service rather than the 'cards being stacked' in favour of the professional's or bureaucrat's influence. This is the creation of the 'consumer-citizen' (Le Grand, 1993, cited in Harris, 1999, p 923). Since 1997, Labour governments have "implicitly accepted the free market to deliver [social welfare] services but this is tempered by centralised regulation" (Malin et al, 2002, p 10). For example, in the NHS the purchaser and provider split was reformed and market competition has been replaced with a duty of cooperation (Malin et al, 2002, pp 3, 10-11).

However, a primary criticism of this consumerist model and marketisation – leading sometimes to privatisation or outsourcing – is its negative implication for social justice. For example, consumer choice in public services provision can be used to mask the operation of other goals, say, by offering consumers something in compensation for cuts being made at the same time. In education, this point has been levelled against school choice and charter school initiatives in the 1990s (Perri 6, 2002, p 244). More fundamentally, the problem is that many 'consumer-citizens' of social welfare services are likely to be "poor, vulnerable, and rarely in a position to shop around or take their custom elsewhere" (Politt, 1990, cited in Harris, 1999, p 926).

Yet 'citizen empowerment' does not necessarily involve the consumerist route. 'Empowerment' may refer to the users of public services choosing an 'exit point' and selecting an alternative service provider – but it can also refer to the ability to 'have a say' and influence in the way services are provided within a system. In this sense, empowerment means "service users have more control or power over the services or support they receive" (Adams, 1996, cited in Malin et al, 2002, p 61).

Key elements might include:

- service-user involvement from the outset in service development;
- users playing a key role in assessing their own situation;
- users having a say in how services are planned, managed and delivered;
- some user control/consultation over the allocation of resources; and
- user contribution to the evaluation of services.

In addition, ICT can play a key supporting role, in particular by providing greater self-access to information on services – including on rights to use, availability of types of delivery and different service options.

Hence, within much social welfare practice, emphasis is placed on shifting empowerment from a consumerist to a democratic perspective. This represents a challenge of moving beyond a "limited notion of consultation or market research" to meaningful and systematic involvement based on social rights of citizenship (Watson, 2002, p 885).

Finally, theories of commodification may, for example, have particular gender, race or disability implications. To take the case of gender, in examining the effects of social security reform in the UK, Mumford (2001, p 418) argues that "the commodification of mothering" is ignored in the changes to the Working Families Tax Credit. The commodification question, in this context, asks "whether classifying household work economically" promotes or detracts from the "quest of achieving equality of opportunity in the workplace".

Chapter Nine will consider the potential of ICT to catalyse – or limit – new forms of citizen involvement.

Advocacy and self-help

At its simplest, advocacy means 'speaking up' for oneself or others. Its origins lie in a radical social welfare critique that "in day-to-day social work people will need someone to mediate between themselves and the formal agencies" (Jordan, 1987, cited in Craig, 1998a, p 12). Advocacy is often linked to promoting user-centred or user-led services and developing partnerships between professionals, users and others (Craig, 1998a, p 13). Advocacy – and closely related counselling and mediation services – are "all voluntary processes which service users can enter or leave at any time" (Craig, 1998b, p 238). ICT can support advocates within social welfare functions in fulfilling the role of (electronic) 'information intermediaries', as will be introduced in Chapter Seven.

'Citizen advocacy' typically involves a one-to-one relationship between a "volunteer spokesperson and their disadvantaged partner" (Atkinson, 1999, p 6). It may be practised by a volunteer citizen or a professional caseworker, forming part of everyday work in health, housing and social care settings (for example, supporting older people with dementia). Advocacy has a strong link with rights and citizenship; hence, a service employing advocacy (as well as other policy development and campaigning) skills is welfare rights in social security, debt and housing issues. 'Self-advocacy' is described as "a process in which an individual, or a group of people, speak or act on their own behalf in pursuit of their own needs and interests" (Bateman, 2000, p 18). It has prominent origins among people using mental health services and those with learning (and, increasingly now, physical) difficulties, in order to influence social policy and welfare practice (Atkinson, 1999, p 6).

The history of advocacy in relation to disabled people, as Atkinson's review shows, is more to do with self-help, combined with self and peer representation. The roots of self-help can be traced to the end of the 19th century, with the formation of the British Deaf Association and the National League of the Blind. In contemporary times, self-help groups and user-led organisations have proliferated, such as the Spinal Injuries Association (Atkinson, 1999, p 11). In *Bowling alone*, Putnam traces the growth in participation in self-help and support groups, from long-established 'twelve-step' organisations – such as Alcoholics Anonymous – to the many support groups relating to specific diseases (such as muscular dystrophy or AIDS) (Putnam, 2000, p 150).

Ideas of advocacy and self-support underlie the use of Internet chat rooms and similar interactive, peer support for citizens, which is outlined in Chapter Four. In Chapter Seven, the way that opportunities for self-help in social welfare are being transformed by ICT will also be considered – for example, the growth of Internet-led medical consumerism. Finally, the implications for social welfare campaigning will be examined in Chapter Nine.

Community development and social capital

There is a strong recognition in social policy of how deprived neighbourhoods reinforce the exclusion of families (Pierson, 2002, p 95). Community development – whether through social work, neighbourhood work, community education or community action – involves working on a wide variety of issues that affect families. These may include drugs, prostitution, homelessness and school truancy or exclusion, as well as encompassing support to individuals and families in establishing, for example, local provision for adult education, a women's refuge or Local Exchange and Trading Systems (LETS) schemes.

Central to the ethos and values of community development work is the fact that services are not simply conceived, planned and delivered by professionals, but are shaped by local people's participation and involvement. This should mean, in theory, that, as well as *outcomes* of new or enhanced service provision, the *process* enhances "the capabilities of individuals to enter into reciprocal exchanges – the basis of a social network" (Canaan, 1992, cited in Pierson, 2002, p 96).

The term 'social capital' is applied to "those features in a community or society which promote cohesion and a sense of 'belonging'" (Cooper et al, 1999, p 2). According to Smythe (2001, pp 1-3), it may be defined, simply, as "the connectivity in society" and includes:

- community involvement and participation;
- community consultation and empowerment;
- community development;
- community groups;
- tenant and resident groups;
- community management and ownership;
- voluntary sector;
- churches and faith groups;
- community representation and governance; and
- community planning.

The relationship between social capital and community development can, therefore, be seen as the latter forming one activity (of many) that "encourag[es] the growth of the former".

In the 1990s, the evolution of the community development approach into a greater focus on promoting social inclusion and social capital is illustrated by a crucial emphasis on addressing physical *and* social aspects of community. For example, in neighbourhood renewal programmes, improving the quality of life of people is partly about the *built environment* in terms of quality of housing, existence of leisure facilities and safety of the public realm. Yet "even more important to understanding the level of exclusion in a locality" is the *social fabric* – social connections between people, the strength of local organisations and associations and the extent and vibrancy of local activity whether commercial or civic (Pierson, 2002, p 14). Hence, social capital is said to exist when three conditions are met –"networks, trust and civic institutions" (Jupp and Bentley, 2001, p 98).

James Coleman ('Social capital in the creation of human capital', 1988) is acknowledged as one of the first popularisers of the concept of 'social capital', followed by Robert Putnam (see Box 2.1). Coleman (1988, cited in Cooper et al, 1999, pp 28-9) used the following measures in the community when investigating the relationship between educational achievement and levels of social capital in the family and wider adult community:

- "the social relationships that exist among parents", relating to information exchange and levels of trust;
- norms of accepted behaviour, and sanctions; and
- affiliation with local organisations.

However, two important criticisms have been levelled against Putnam's analysis. First, his measures may have underestimated the effect on social capital of women taking their leadership and organisational skills from civic activity into

Box 2.1: Putnam and social capital

Many social scientists now accept Putnam's definition of social capital – "the features of social organisations, such as networks, norms, and social trust that facilitate coordination and cooperation for mutual benefit". His main thesis is that since the end of the 1940s in the US there has been a decline in individual levels of social trust, accompanied by a corresponding decline in group affiliation, which indicates an overall decline in social capital. He sees social capital as a 'moral resource', supplies of which increase with use – the higher the level, the easier it is for people to work together for the common good. In turn, the "more people work together, the more social capital is produced". It is a 'public good', like air, and so cannot be commodified. Underpinning this model, he identifies a positive correlation between social participation and tolerance, especially with respect to gender and race. Across all levels of income, Putnam finds that there had been a reduction in trust and participation and hence civic engagement. He has discovered that dependence on television for entertainment is "the single most consistent predictor" of civic disengagement, since it "privatizes our civic activity" by reducing collective activities – like attending public meetings – by as much as 40%.

Sources: Cooper et al (1999, pp 24, 32-3, 35-6); Putnam (2000, pp 229, 231)

the workplace (Skocpol, 1996, cited in Cooper et al, 1999, p 36). Second, his measures overlook 'single issue' civic activity, which is likely to entail more occasional involvement (Schudson, 1996, cited in Cooper et al, 1999, p 36). On the latter point, Putnam (2000, p 160) counters that such organisations "provide neither connectedness among members nor direct engagement in civic give-and-take".

The notion of communities of interest was introduced in Chapter One, and, in this section, the broader concept was considered of how *the community* – made up of a range of communities of interest – can be supported by social welfare professionals and practitioners. In Chapter Four, the role of ICT in making possible 'virtual communities' will be shown. "The creation of bridging social capital [is now recognised as] a particularly important and beneficial activity" for "reviving local democracy and encouraging volunteers and active citizens" (Smythe, 2001, pp 5-6). In Chapter Nine, social capital is revisited in terms of its implications for campaigns, communities and communication.

The remainder of this chapter will focus on two critical concerns with ICT – relating to confidentiality and child safety – on the part of both users and professionals.

Confidentiality

Role of confidentiality in professional cultures

The concept of confidentiality in information collection, storage and usage is central to the ethos and practice of social welfare. In essence, personal details of the client that are obtained by professionals and practitioners are held to be private and not to be shared beyond the direct needs of that support or intervention. Exceptions do exist, for example, in child protection, in which the welfare of the child or young person is considered paramount and may therefore override parents' confidentiality of, say, their social security or medical data (1989 Children Act).

There is a difficult balance to be achieved between promoting online services and ensuring confidentiality of data. There will clearly be some areas of social welfare provision in which electronic service delivery (ESD) is not regarded as appropriate. According to the Office of the e-Envoy, such areas included the work of the National Probation Service, victim support and asylum-seeking claims in 2002 (Office of the e-Envoy, 2002, p 3). In most other social welfare areas, there is now a strong imperative that "sharing personal information between partner agencies is vital to the provision of co-ordinated and seamless care to an individual" (Clark, 2000, p 13). While technology can allow for proper safeguards to be instituted, barriers to inter-agency information sharing across ICT systems persist.

These include the contribution of the role of different professional cultures. In a social housing and social care research study on ESD, IT and non-front-line staff were most likely to feel that "data protection was sometimes used as a smokescreen ... [by front-line staff] who were reluctant to lose control of their data and autonomy". In other words, they saw this as the result of 'professional specialisms' rather than a real obstacle (Pleace and Quilgars, 2002, p 31).

Indeed, issues of confidentiality have to be addressed within single social welfare agencies even before the challenges of inter-agency information sharing are considered. The NHS provides an example through the development of secure e-mail within its intranet, *NHSmail* (see Box 2.2).

With information exchange between agencies, difficulties often arise in reconciling different professional cultures' understanding of confidentiality requirements. Attitudes and values become entrenched through years of training and practice, as well as ongoing monitoring (through management supervision) and audit (by government inspection or professional bodies). Although data safeguards are integral to the work of all social welfare practitioners and professionals, the full apparatus of rules and standards for ensuring confidentiality may have higher thresholds in certain areas – social care, medicine, police – than in others.

For example, how can the routine sharing of medical information with social services and the police in child protection be limited (when this may not be directly relevant to current concerns) in a context of recent tragedies arising

Box 2.2: NHSmail

NHSmail aims to provide a mail service that NHS staff will want to use and that is free for NHS organisations at the point of delivery. Once they have registered for the new service, NHS employees – from health visitors to clinic clerks, and from GPs to physiotherapists – will be able to send and pick up e-mails wherever there is a web browser. The new e-mail service has the approval of the British Medical Association for clinical messaging, provided it is used in a way that satisfies its joint guidelines with the NHS (*Using NHSmail for clinical communications*). The high level of security on NHSmail means that for the first time clinical e-mails can be safely used to replace paper-based communications where 'structured messaging' is not practical, such as patient referrals, discharge letters or clinical enquiries. For these applications, clinical information produced on word processors can be sent as attachments to e-mails on NHSmail, securely encrypted.

Source: NHSIA (2003)

from ineffective communication of such information between agencies (Valios, 2002, p 32)? Hence, the UK government, for its Green Paper *Every child matters*, consulted professionals and the public on how "to prevent situations where a child does not receive the help they need because of too rigid an interpretation of the privacy of the child and their family" (DfES, 2003a, p 54).

UK legislation: a tension

The UK government has recognised that electronic services can "heighten public concern about the security of transactions and about who gets to see and share their private information" (ODPM, 2002, p 23). Yet there is conflicting legislation relating to the security and safeguarding of information on the one hand and freedom of information on the other. The 1998 Data Protection Act – in force in the UK since March 2000 – applies to virtually all organisations. It requires agencies to provide citizens with details of who is processing their data and for what purpose, including, in some cases, obtaining subjects' consent to process the data. This will nearly always be required in cases of sensitive data relating to health or criminal records.

The implications affect social welfare organisations particularly in relation to day-to-day operational data in service provision. In many functions, staff will also need to have some training or briefings on the organisations' data protection policies and practices. Appropriate security systems, for both electronic and 'hard copy' data, need to be established and monitored. Voluntary sector fundraising departments have to build in ways of offering people the choice of opting out of any direct marketing.

The key elements of the Act are set out in Box 2.3.

> ## Box 2.3: Key elements of the 1998 Data Protection Act
>
> Personal data must:
>
> - be processed fairly and lawfully;
> - be obtained only for specified purposes, and then must not be used for anything else;
> - be adequate, relevant and not excessive;
> - be accurate and, where necessary, kept up to date;
> - not be kept longer than necessary;
> - be processed in accordance with the rights of data subjects;
> - be protected using appropriate technical and organisational security measures to be taken; and
> - be transferred outside western Europe (or put on the Internet) only if certain conditions are met.
>
> *Source:* Ticher and Powell (2000, p 109)

By January 2005, under the 2000 Freedom of Information Act, individual UK citizens will be guaranteed access to all information held by government, statutory bodies and health service providers. The Act establishes access as a general right and shifts to public bodies responsibility for justifying any withholding of requested information. Accordingly, social welfare and other public services will have to meet these obligations to release information alongside existing confidentiality laws and agreements. For example, if someone requests a council document that contains identifying information about a third person, this could fall under the Data Protection Act and be exempt from freedom of information requirements (Parkinson, 2003b). Again, in the introduction of information, referral and tracking (IRT) systems (see the case study in Chapter Five) the core application of a shared children's database in local areas has come up against confidentiality barriers. Legal concerns have been raised in relation to the Data Protection Act and the Human Rights Act (Article 8, 'right to respect for private and family life') (Batty, 2003, p 10).

In November 2003, the UK government published a key document to provide legal guidance on *Data sharing in the public sector* (Department of Constitutional Affairs, 2003). There is also guidance on establishing data-sharing protocols, which will support agencies involved in such new schemes as IRT systems. It is intended that the department's website (www.dca.gov.uk) will be an updated resource for professionals and will include a library of good practice.

Finally, the privacy and data protection concerns of citizens may not, of course, apply only to public sector services. Charities are keen to extend their fundraising initiatives based on text messaging (SMS) direct to donors' mobile phones. However, they are being held back because "confusion surrounds the legal status of unsolicited text messages", since this form of telecommunications is not actually covered by the Data Protection Act. It was expected that an EU directive would bring new rules into force in autumn 2003 (Parsons, 2002).

The citizen perspective on privacy

In the past two decades, a curious paradox has become apparent. On the one hand, the public is less apprehensive when data is collected, say through everyday credit card transactions, which are "perceived as convenient and beneficial". On the other hand, the use of personal data is still "frequently regarded as risky and needing regulation when it involves government" (Raab et al, 1996, pp 293-4). Citizens are now realising that they were mistaken in the belief that they could hand over so much information to government agencies "precisely because they assumed that government was incapable of collating it" (Cairncross, 2001, pp 166-7).

The UK government has made a clear statement that "it may be technically possible to share information, but it will only be legal and acceptable with the consent of the citizens concerned" (ODPM, 2002, p 23). This position accepts that the take-up of public and social welfare services by ESD will "depend heavily upon the citizen's trust in the online relationship with government" (Kearns et al, 2002, p 30).

This lack of trust on the part of citizens may derive from fears about erosions of privacy under a 'Big Brother' government and anxieties about censorship. Should free expression through the Internet have any limits? Or is some element of government censorship necessary to guard against 'cyberterrorism'? Would citizens want their government to be prohibited from helping to protect against global computer viruses; to control violent and child pornography images; or to ban speech that contains direct threats of violence aimed at particular people (including doctors in the abortion field, ethnic or religious groups) (Sunstein, 2002, pp 127-8, 134, 159-61)?

In many advanced economies, governments know far more about their citizens than do any private companies, through the networked computer leaving behind 'a thick trail of data' every time people conduct online transactions. Increasingly, integrated ICT systems hold personal data on health, crime, social security, vehicle registration and so forth, which can be cross-referenced. This is despite the fact that, when governments collect such data, they generally use it in ways to promote citizens' welfare – such as tackling traffic jams, detecting crime and safeguarding vulnerable groups. In general terms, a survey in the US found that 87% of Americans had such concerns (Cairncross, 2001, pp 225, 228). More specifically, in the UK, when the public were asked, "To whom are you happy to offer full access to your medical records?", it was found that hospital doctors and consultants received a rating of 83% but social care staff just 23% (NHS Information Authority survey, 'Share with care', October 2002, cited in Poluck, 2003a).

Public distrust may also relate more to concerns about the (in)efficiency of public sector bodies in safeguarding the personal information they collect and hold (Raab et al, 1996, p 293). In a research study, users – including older people in sheltered housing, young people living in foyers and people with mental health problems – were consulted about ESD in the social housing and social care fields. "There was a widespread concern that confidential information given to a computer was inherently insecure", thereby acting as a strong disincentive for their use of ESD (Pleace and Quilgars, 2002, p 47).

This paradox in the public's attitudes towards privacy may unravel when the public feels that government's use of ICT "deliver[s] real personal benefits" (Raab et al, 1996, pp 293-4). In the near future, this may be judged through the greater use of 'smart cards', potentially giving citizens access to a range of public and private services with just one card (Office of the e-Envoy, 2003b). In the meantime, the UK government is developing a Public Services Trust Charter to promote the main principles of the Data Protection Act and set out the key commitments to be adhered to by the public sector when handling personal data. This recognises that, if ICT routes for obtaining social welfare information and services are to be taken up, public trust must be prioritised just as much as the infrastructure needed for connectivity, public awareness and accessibility (Lowe, 2003).

Themes of confidentiality and privacy will return in Chapter Nine, in terms of the significance of growing 'convergence' in ICT – and across welfare planning and media – for government surveillance and the undermining of privacy.

Internet safety concerns for children and young people

A key element of many citizens' and professionals' concerns about the unrestricted use of ICT relates to two interlinked child protection concerns of Internet safety. First, there is the issue of access to certain images on the Internet by children and young people. Second, children are also vulnerable to paedophile activity through the latter's exploitation of ICT, particularly the Internet and now also other ICT platforms. Confidentiality and privacy factors are relevant, too, in these debates.

There need to be safeguards for children and young people's access to online pornographic (and violent, racist or anti-gay) website material. A 2001 survey found that 70% of young people had "accidentally stumbled across pornography online", with 19% "very upset" by the experience (Hughes et al, 2002, p 89). They are most likely to access the Internet at home, typically in an unfiltered and unsupervised environment. Indeed, research commissioned by the DfES in 2002 found that two thirds of the time that children spend online is unsupervised (BBC News, 2002a).

The use of filtering software is a popular method for parents and professionals to try to keep children safe from unsuitable Internet content. Some of the most powerful programmes can monitor the sites children visit and what they say in chat rooms or on e-mail (Harris, 2003, p 7). Yet defects across a range of such software products were identified in an evaluation study by Parents Information Network (Krechowiecka, 2001). In addition, while filtering software may be effective in blocking undesirable material, it may also prevent young people's access to vital social welfare information and guidance, for example, on sex education or breast cancer, through its crude recognition of keywords common to pornographic sites (Naughton, 2003a). Nevertheless, the Children's Charities Coalition for Internet Safety is lobbying the UK government for the compulsory pre-installation of child protection software (Maler, 2003).

Technological advance means that dangers have arisen from 'picture messaging' functions (via built-in cameras) in two thirds of mobile phones now produced. Most of these models also allow users direct access to the Internet. These phones can be used by paedophiles in swimming pools and leisure centres, and – particularly with prepaid mobile phones – anonymity can be maintained when the images are sent, via 'picture messaging', to a network of paedophiles. International research has highlighted the dangers of paedophiles exploiting children's increasingly widespread ownership of these mobile phones by getting them to record and transmit pictures of themselves naked (Wray, 2003; A. Hill, 2003).

The second major area in which protective measures are required is paedophile activity in developing contact with children and young people through the Internet, known as online 'grooming'. A MORI survey for the NSPCC showed that more than nine in 10 adults are worried about sex offenders logging on to Internet chat rooms in order to gain access to children (NSPCC, 2003). In a cross-European research study (UK, Ireland and Greece), worryingly low levels of awareness of key Internet safety messages were found. One in two chat users was unaware of the guidelines 'always take an adult to a face-to-face meeting' and 'always meet in a public place'. One in five chat users was also unaware that "people may be lying about their identity" (Safer Internet, 2003e).

"The arrival of strong encryption technologies adds considerably to [the Internet's] risks" as a conduit for 'grooming' activity by sex offenders (NSPCC, 2000). Recent media coverage has shown that Internet 'peer-to-peer' file-sharing services are being used by paedophiles to exchange images of children. Over a six-week period, NSPCC research monitored more than 140,000 child pornography images being posted on the Internet (Safer Internet, 2003f). 'Peer-to-peer' refers to the fact that files are located on and transferred by easily accessed, downloadable software used by millions of users for a wide variety of purposes (including the distribution of music files). The problem is largely 'hidden' because there is no central server that could be closed down or raided for information to identify users of the service.

Current legislative proposals in the UK (2003 Sexual Offences Bill, clauses 8, 10, 11, 13 and 17) introduce a specific offence relating to the 'grooming' of children on the Internet, which would address a legal loophole in sentencing following several high-profile cases (Barnardo's et al, 2003, pp 1-2; Bowcott, 2003; Vasager, 2003, p 7). An alternative approach is to censor content on the Internet itself in order to protect vulnerable end users. If the creation, distribution or storage of information or content is outlawed, it is irrelevant whether that content is digital and stored on a hard drive or in printed form. Another form of control lies in the caution exercised by mainstream Internet service providers (ISPs) hosting websites. In their user licence agreements, ISPs now usually reserve the right to withdraw services from those choosing to upload content that is either illegal or may be considered offensive. One major chat room provider, MSN, took high-profile action in October 2003 by closing all its UK chat rooms in order to help safeguard children (Carter, 2003).

Yet there are two main practical difficulties with a policy of content censorship. First, the technology is rapidly developing so that where users wish to hide themselves as originators or distributors of illegal content, they effectively can. Second, it appears to be difficult for criminal justice and legal systems to keep up with the rate of evolution in technology to ensure effective regulation and enforcement. This is compounded by the global context of the Internet and the large number of different legal frameworks. In short, irrespective of the ethics of censorship, these factors militate against any hope of effective policing of 'banned material' that would be acceptable in the context of a liberal democracy.

Ultimately, therefore, Internet safety solutions by governments, social welfare agencies, the ICT industry and parents must try to achieve a trade-off of "freedoms against safety ... guiding children towards valuable uses of the Internet while also teaching them safety awareness" (Livingstone, 2001, p 12). Too great an emphasis on control and censorship may be detrimental to the necessity of the development of ICT skills in the young as a preparation for adult working and cultural life, as well as to the broader civil liberties of citizens.

Thinklist

- **How important is information in the provision of your services?**
- **The 1998 Data Protection Act is frequently misunderstood. What are the main principles underlying the Act (see www.informationcommissioner.gov.uk)? Should you change your practice?**
- **What is the range of mechanisms to protect children, and adults, from exposure to offensive material and potential dangers of abuse on the Internet?**

THREE

Putting the I and the C back into ICT

Introduction

Information is a precursor to effective decision making; therefore information is one of the single most important aspects of social welfare practice. Indeed, the use of information in social welfare is so ubiquitous that practitioners give the concept of information per se little attention.

This chapter:

- demonstrates that information is a product in its own right and has independent value to service users and staff, and then explores the issues flowing from this;
- explores the concept of knowledge management and links it to the concepts of life-long learning and the learning organisation;
- examines some basic models of information management: its gathering, management, storage and retrieval, and transmission;
- identifies some common anxieties in relation to ICT in these processes; and
- describes three information models.

The importance of information

Laming (1998, para 3.4, p 20) wrote in relation to social services: "Good information is essential to help users and the public in general find out about what is available and so make informed and rational choices". The provision of information for service users is vital in the fields of welfare rights (for example, Walker, 2003), employment services (Ducatel et al, 2000b), and health – as was seen in the example of NHS Direct – and good information is part of good healthcare.

Information has value independently of the context from which it springs – as educationalists, librarians, marketers and the media well know. A helpful distinction here is that between information content and information carrier. Content can be defined as the information per se, while the carrier is the mechanism by which the information is stored and conveyed. In technical terminology, the term 'channel' is used for 'carrier'. Thus, the same *content* can go via the different *channels* of book, radio, newspaper, and so on.

If it is accepted that information and knowledge have independent value, there is no reason why this understanding should not be applied to social welfare. Indeed, certain areas of social welfare devote considerable resources to using this insight. Public health promotion campaigns are perhaps the most visible, but recent campaigns highlighting new benefits (for example, the Working Families Tax Credit) (*Sun*, 2003) have also adopted an approach around the transmission of information. Indeed, "the planned and sustained effort to establish and maintain goodwill and understanding between an organisation and its publics" (Harrison, 1995, p 2) is essential for all social welfare organisations. Information is central to the tasks of advocacy and campaigning and to the educative aspects of welfare.

The very omnipresence of information means that its characteristics and therefore the management and application of information are not as well understood as they might be. Dutton states: "Information is data that has been organised and communicated" (Dutton, 2001). The context of information is important in adding meaning (Junnarkar, 2002, p 31). An example of this is the postal address – perhaps one of the most frequently gathered 'atoms' of information in social welfare practice. By itself an address means little. However, in context, an address can mean a lot. Thus, experience of the local geographical area might lead a police officer or a benefit officer to know that the address given does not in fact exist, for the social worker a certain address might convey the socioeconomic context of a family, for a community worker an address might signal the presence or absence of a wider community group as a resource (of 'social capital') for the family to draw on.

Information comes in a wide range of shapes and forms and is gathered, managed, stored, retrieved and transmitted by a broad range of methods. Figure 3.1 attempts to convey this by using a sample of differing practitioner groups and setting out the similarities and differences in gathering, managing and transmitting information.

As can be seen from Figure 3.1, information is a *resource* and a *tool*. It enables specific tasks to be undertaken. Indeed, information is a precursor to action. Information can often have a 'sell-by date'; that is, it may be required only for a specific deadline, after which it is has limited value. After all, who is prepared to buy yesterday's newspaper? The transmission of information, then, can be a valuable action in itself if it gets to the right place at the right time. Those who work in fields of social welfare where speedy assessment and intervention are of the essence (healthcare, child protection, crime reduction) know this well.

All too often these basic 'atoms' – the building blocks of information - may be lacking. One author remembers taking up a new post in a department that had experienced a sudden haemorrhage of long-serving staff. It was discovered that although all the clients had extensive case files, most of the files had no client address or telephone number. Consequently, the first few days were lost spent tracking down the contact details of the clients. Some days later it was realised this was because the previous staff had kept the client contact details in their personal address books. But this experience is not unique.

Figure 3.1: Similarities and differences in information handling

Methods of informal handling / Type of social welfare work	Gathered by ...	Stored, managed and retrieved by	Transmitted by ...	Resulting in decision, action ...
Benefits Officer	• Claimant application form • Benefits handbook • Face-to-face interview • Documenta-tion, eg P45	• Brain • Case file • Database	• Letter • Face-to-face contact • Telephone	Decision about claim
Child Protection Social Worker	• Neighbour • Family member • Child/parent • Inter-agency referral • Inter-agency consultation • Seeing child/ home visit • School contact	• Brain • Case file • Database	• Face-to-face contact with family • Letters/ telephone • Multi-agency Case Conference	Decision about needs of child
Community worker	• Public meeting • Newspaper • Initiation by community • Community needs assessment	• Brain • File	• Public meeting • Community publications • Website/e-mail • Text message	Decision about how to work with community in respect of the issue
Voluntary sector fundraiser	• Trust or Foundation information in directory or website • Approach by Trust or Foundation • Informal networks • Charity circuit	• Brain • File • Personal notes • Database	• Funding application form completed	Application by funder accepted or rejected
Health practitioner	• Direct consultation with patient • Previous medical records • Clinical tests • Medical reference books	• Brain • Clinical file • Clinical records on database	• Direct consultation with patient • Letter	Decision about health status of patient

In relation to:

- the police it was reported that the Police National Computer was in some areas up to six months out of date affecting decisions about risk to the public, arrest and crime reporting and probation (*BBC News; Today*, 10 Feb, 2003);
- the social services: "'... both inspections and joint reviews repeatedly find that service users have not received timely and helpful information" (Laming, 1998, p 20); and,
- the NHS missing and incomplete health information (Audit Commission, 2002).

To help understand these problems, a basic lexicon is useful. Information can be classified as tacit or explicit. "Tacit information is personal, context specific, and therefore hard to formalise and communicate" (Takeuchi and Ikujiro, 1995, p 141). Practitioners and professionals routinely hold large amounts of information over and above more prosaic chunks of information held by the organisation. Often long-serving staff can be a gold mine of information resources, including:

- the historic context of decisions that continue to affect the present;
- personal quirks of managers that drive specific decisions;
- alternative sources of advice and information;
- friendly individuals and contacts in other agencies who are prepared to 'go the extra mile';
- agencies with specialist expertise and/or resources;
- techniques to bypass bureaucratic sclerosis and so forth.

Tacit knowledge may not be recognised by the individual let alone by the social welfare organisation that employs that individual. In contrast, "[e]xplicit knowledge ...refers to knowledge that is transmittable in formal, systematic language" (Takeuchi and Ikujiro, 1995, p 141).

Information can be further categorised as 'formal' – those tangible manifestations of information in the organisation (such as the memo, the e-mail, the case file, the policy guidelines, the legislation, the finance procedures) – or as 'informal' – those categories of information that staff acquire through chance meetings or gossip, and carry in their heads and in the jottings and recordings in diaries, notebooks, audio tapes and other means of storage (Daniels, 1994, pp 33-4). The terms 'formal' and 'informal' should not be equated with 'effective' and 'ineffective': often informal systems are highly effective and some formal systems are highly ineffective. These informal categories supplement – or can even substitute for – the formal categories of information. As Heeks and Bhatnagar (Heeks, 1999, p 63) put it:

Detailed studies show again and again that the real decision making processes of organisations … rely extensively on informal information (Daft and Lengel, 1986; Hastings, 1996; Heckscher, 1994). Research in UK public service organisations by Davies (1997), for example, demonstrates the importance of personal contacts, 'invisible colleges' and face-to-face meetings both in the normal operation of these organisations and during processes of reform. Informal information is valued because, compared with formal information, it often:

- provides more background and explanatory detail;
- enables a fuller evaluation of the consequences of decision alternatives;
- is more timely;
- is easier to interrogate for further details;
- better serves personal objectives and interests.

Information can often migrate from informal and tacit models to formal and explicit ones; this process can be bottom-up or top-down or a combination of the two. Thus, in terms of bottom-up initiatives it is not uncommon that staff, over a period of time, have evolved a system, a pattern of what goes where: all the files beginning with 'A' go in this drawer, all the rent payments go into this file, all the oversize books in the library go in this shelf. Generally, the smaller the team, the slower the turnover of staff, the smaller the volume of work, and the more straightforward the tasks, the more staff can rely on an evolutionary formalisation. Thus, practice about 'what is stored where' is reflected in a document, custom and practice are reflected in staff handbooks, and so forth. Other bottom-up models involve practitioners developing personal files, small professional libraries and other personal resources. Sometimes these resources are held at the workplace, sometimes at home. Not for nothing have some labelled these practitioners as knowledge workers – see Chapter Two (Webb, 2003, p 235).

Developing a system to log tacit and informal information is particularly hard. The solution might lie in the weblog; a shared website on which notes can be written, documents pasted and sound and film attached. Because it is a shared resource, it can reflect a variety of contributions.

The value of informal and tacit information is often unrecognised in social welfare organisations, which is ironic since many of these organisations would pride themselves of being 'people organisations'. Unlike manufacturing or commerce, in which considerable assets are deployed (in manufacturing) and cash (in commerce), the assets of social welfare organisations consist wholly of the staff. David Ogilvy, advertising guru, was reputed to have said of his firm: "All our assets go home every night". The same is true of social welfare organisations. Consequently, some parts of the private sector have attempted to value this intangible resource in cash terms. Thus, a valuation of Microsoft argued that the company was 'worth' $80 billion-$90 billion based on the 'know-how' held collectively in staff heads, whereas the physical assets of

Microsoft on their own were worth 'merely' $1 billion (Mulgan, 1998, p 214). Often these 'valuations' can be grossly overstated, reflecting some ulterior motive, but the basic ideas that significant assets are held in staff heads and that their value needs to be formally recognised must be sound. One benefit is that it means *all* staff, not just the top management, are valued for their accumulated wisdom.

An organisation's efforts to systematise and develop tacit and informal information into explicit and formal information may involve an attempt at knowledge management:

> Knowledge Management is a discipline that promotes an integrated approach to identifying, managing and sharing all of an enterprise's information assets, including databases, documents, policies and procedures as well as unarticulated expertise and experience resident in individual workers. (Gartner Group, cited in Morey et al, 2002, p xii)

> The success of a knowledge organisation depends on its ability to gather information and knowledge, to integrate it into existing organisational knowledge, to share and leverage it, and to apply it to create value for clients. (Stahle, 2002, p 10)

The danger with this kind of approach is that it can be perceived as 'sucking out' the staff's skills so that they can subsequently be discarded by the organisation.

A model that incorporates the idea of knowledge management but has a more 'friendly face' is the 'learning organisation'. This model is linked to the concept of lifelong learning, which is predicated on the assumption that, since change (both in practice and in policy) is a given of modern society, the organisation and those who work in it need to ensure the opportunity for constant development:

> In the Learning Age we will need a workforce with imagination and confidence, and the skills required will be diverse.... All of these occupations … demand different types of knowledge and understanding and the skills to apply them. That is what we mean by skills, and it is through learning – with the help of those who teach us – that we acquire them. (DfEE, 1998, p 13, cited in Jarvis, 2002)

"Organisational learning is the process by which organisations generate and diffuse knowledge" (Senge, 2002); thus, the learning organisation adapts successfully to its changing environment.

These models of knowledge management and lifelong learning are also reflected in attempts to develop information resources that support practitioner and professional development and are independent of particular employers both at the national level (for example, the National Electronic Library for

Health/Social Care Institute for Excellence [SCIE] at www.scie.org.uk) and the global level (for example, via the World Health Organization; Gould, 2003). This type of education is sometimes described as 'e-learning'.

In contrast, the organisation that fails to learn can be said to be condemned to repeat the same mistakes. One is reminded of the mistakes made in relation to the deaths of the children Jasmine Beckford in the mid-1980s and subsequently in relation to Victoria Climbié. As the Social Services Inspectorate put it: "The Victoria Climbié Inquiry reinforced [the knowledge] that effective information systems are essential for safeguarding children" (DoH/SSI, 2003, p 1).

Information and ICT

ICT is *one* technical apparatus for carrying out the tasks of handling information (Daniels, 1994, p 32). It is one carrier (channel) of content among many carriers (channels) of content. However, ICT models have taken an increasingly predominant role in handling information. This is because ICT can:

- automate routine tasks, thus freeing up labour for more productive roles (for example, payroll);
- sort and collate routine information accurately in ways that would be very labour intensive to do manually (such as database searches);
- give multiple users access to the same information simultaneously and from a remote location (whereas individual copies of paper information can be read by only one person in one place);
- secure information by providing fully accurate copies at almost zero cost (for instance, databases can be copied and stored safely off-site, whereas there is usually only one set of paper files, which, if destroyed, is lost for ever); and
- enable communication and broadcasting of information quickly and cheaply (for example, e-mail and websites).

In short, ICT systems can provide benefits that are cheaper, quicker, more effective and more accurate than paper-based or mental systems (Heeks, 1999, p 18).

Information held on ICT systems has some unique characteristics. Generally speaking, the more individuals who own the same product, the less it is worth to any one individual. Thus, someone who owns a car can use it every day of the year. If the car is co-owned by 364 other people, use may be restricted to one day a year. Not so with information. If that person owns an e-mail address and no one else possesses it, it is worthless. If 364 other people know that address, it becomes extremely valuable to that individual. If all 364 individuals also know 364 addresses, the value of the network is even higher. In technical terms, this phenomenon is known as 'connectivity' or 'network effects' (Castells, 2001, p 100). The possibilities of using this model to bring about national (and international change) are explored in Chapter Nine.

However, the increasing use of ICT in information handling gives rise to some anxieties among some groups and individuals:

- Many social welfare practitioners place a high premium on face-to-face contact, and the use of various media to reach service users independent of professionals can be seen as problematic (for example, see Huntington and Sapey, 2003).
- The introduction of new unfamiliar technologies gives rise to concerns around breach of confidentiality. But as Gould puts it:

    the ... view which sees the computerisation of services as a threat to confidentiality rests upon the rather questionable assumption that information is more likely to be breached if stored electronically than if maintained on paper. (Gould, 2003, p 42)

- Chapter One introduced the concept of disintermediation (Evans and Wurster, 2000). Some professionals fear the possibility of being literally 'cut out of the loop' (see, for example, Regan, 2003; Webb, 2003).

Seeing the provision of information as a service – whether by leaflet or advertisement, or electronically – can produce anxieties for professionals. Anxieties and problems involved in using these 'impersonal methods' of reaching service users are set out in Box 3.1.

Box 3.1: Some common concerns about 'impersonal means' of reaching service users

- The issues are too complex to boil down to simplistic terms.
- Impersonal means of information delivery might result in social welfare practitioners failing to identify the problems experienced by service users.
- Service users do not really want impersonal provision of information.
- The information will be out of date.
- Custom and practice require that services should not be provided this way.
- The cost of transmission by impersonal means can be prohibitive.

In response it might be argued that:

- The provision of information by impersonal means is certainly not perfect or comprehensive; but then neither is the provision of information face-to-face. The provision of information by impersonal means certainly requires specific skills. But in most areas of life others are relied on to simplify complex material.
- The non-identification of problems is a risk. However, face-to-face encounters cannot guarantee that problems are identified or, if identified, appropriately acted upon.
- The preferences of service users are debatable. Experience of the past is not necessarily a good guide to the future.

- It is certainly true that some information will be out of date. Leaflets, for example, can be in circulation well after their 'sell-by date'. However, information provided face-to-face can be frequently out of date too. While a leaflet can be 'date-stamped', a verbal briefing from a staff member can be up to date or it might reflect professional knowledge that is out of date.
- Social policy and social welfare practice is a comparatively new discipline. Nevertheless, history is littered with changes of custom and practice.
- The provision of information by impersonal means is not prohibitively costly but in fact remarkably cheap. It is argued by some that it is more cost-effective to use impersonal means of social welfare support than traditional professional approaches (Byrne, 1997).

But within these organisations, whatever the general trend, the role of individuals remains central. Individual responses range from "I did not come into social work to become a computer operator" (Schofield, 2003) to:

> In those departments where information management was most developed, there was invariably also one or more very able individual ('information champions') who were promoting and enabling good management of information.... (DoH/SSI, 2003, p 24)

Of course, in encouraging staff to use ICT it helps if staff actually have access to it – and many social welfare organisations do not provide this. According the SSI, in 2003 only 54% of front-line social work staff had access to e-mail at work (p 29).

Information systems and information management systems

An information system is quite simply a way of arranging information in an effective way. This is a model that will be developed in the course of this book, but the first place to start thinking about information management systems is a personal information audit (see Box 3.2).

Not having a personal information system can lead to problems. Finding 30 e-mails, 10 letters and five voice mails – as well as a pile of unread reports – when one arrives at the office is increasingly common: a phenomenon graphically described as 'information overload' (Bawden, 2001). An inability to manage this deluge can lead, at best, to that nagging sense of 'something left undone' or, at worst, to severe mental stress.

Clarity about information helps improve communication in terms of who is informed, when they are informed, and how they are informed. Comparatively new forms of ICT lead to people making major communication mistakes. Simply put, they use the wrong channels for the content. Some examples are set out in Box 3.3.

Box 3.2: Personal information systems: an audit

At work and at short notice:

- Can I find a piece of information?
- Do I know where to store a particular piece of information?
- Could appropriate colleagues have access to the information if I were not available?
- Would the information be safe and secure from individuals who should not have access to this information?

The next part of the exercise is to apply these questions to the team of immediate colleagues.

Box 3.3: Some classic communication mistakes

- Sending e-mails to the person next door when a person should simply talk.
- Making inappropriate comments in e-mails that are then quoted in industrial tribunals.
- Circulating e-mails and attachments to large numbers of people who simply do not need to know.
- Dumping huge amounts of text on websites in the belief this aids consultation.
- Undervaluing individuals by texting important content (for example, service cuts).
- Telephone conferencing when face-to-face contact would help establish better rapport.

All information systems need a regular input of resources to make sure they are up to date. This is true of the personal address book (people change their addresses) and the personal diary (meeting dates and venues change) as well as of the most complex organisation–wide ICT systems. Given the importance of the observation that all information systems need sustained and proactive work to maintain their validity, this book adopts the term 'information management systems' because it conveys the idea that the system has to be *actively* managed; a system should not be established and then ignored. An information management system, then, is: "the range of methods and techniques by which information is gathered, managed, stored, retrieved and transmitted before being acted upon" (Heeks, 1999, p 15).

The next task is to start to explore how ICT can effectively support information management systems.

Some models of information

As has already been shown, information is both a tool and a resource. Different practitioners and different professionals need different tools and different resources, and consequently gather, manage, store and retrieve and transmit information for different purposes (Bellamy and Taylor, 1998). Therefore there is no one model of information management. Even within a practitioner or professional group, different levels of staff will seek differing types of information appropriate to their tasks in the organisation. As was demonstrated in Chapter One in relation to cultures and sub-cultures, the larger and more complex the organisation is, the more complex the task will be. A variety of approaches to the issue will be set out in this and subsequent chapters. But a good starting point is to look at some basic building blocks – some different models of information.

Nolan (1987) developed a six-stage model that companies pass through as they grapple with ICT. The six stages are: initiation, contagion, control, integration, data administration and maturity. Initiation reflects the first stage of automation – for example, the payroll and other accounting tools. Meanwhile, falling ICT prices, ever more attractive packages and increasing general knowledge about ICT leads to contagion – superficial enthusiasm for all things ICT-related within the organisation. This phase is characterised by a plethora of ICT systems that are often incompatible with each other. A great deal of staff time is spent on ICT systems – not always effectively – and many avoidable mistakes are made (for example, sets of data are lost because systems are not backed up). Eventually, senior management steps in to centralise hardware and software purchasing (to try to ensure compatibility), formal training systems are instituted and policies and procedures are drawn up. Control has arrived. Integration marks the next step, in which formal information management systems planning begins to coordinate the different systems. Eventually, real benefits start to be realised – maturity.

The second helpful model is Ahituv and Neumann's operational/tactical/ strategic continuum (Ahituv and Neumann, 1987). Information can be categorised as operational, tactical and strategic. Operational information is that used on a regular (for example, daily) basis, tactical is that which informs decision making on a regular but less frequent basis (for example, monthly) while strategic is that which informs decision making on a regular – but infrequent – basis (for example, yearly). In ICT terms, a good example would be accounting software with an interactive link to the bank. The software is used on a daily basis to see whether cheques have cleared (operational), and on a monthly (tactical) basis a check is performed to see whether the different elements of the budget are meeting expected projections and an analysis performed. The information produced by the software will feed into the long-term annual strategic review about the positioning and sustainability of the organisation (strategic). Each tier draws on the information in the tier below.

Depending on personal circumstances, different individuals and teams will have different priorities for operational, tactical or strategic issues.

The third helpful model is to visualise the horizontal and vertical dynamics of the way information is held and the directions in which it flows. Graphic representations of information requirements and flows within an organisation or team are a very helpful way of analysing information management system requirements (Daniels, 1994, p 32). Information is often held in what might be described as 'vertical silos', usually corresponding to the main functional objectives of the organisation, such as finance, property, service-user contact details, human resources, outputs and so forth. Information flows up and down the vertical silos but less frequently across them. Thus, operational financial information flows up to the chief finance officer. However, information is frequently held in a manner that makes it difficult to relate one column to another. So, for example, although a plethora of information may be collected and managed, the relationship between outputs and cost, or between the numbers of staff and the numbers of clients may not always be clear. Without this integration, decision making at the top of the organisation will be seriously impaired since the information available will lack context. Thus, the 'horizontal' flow of information can be quite weak compared with the strong 'vertical' flow of information. The task, then, is to integrate these 'vertical' information systems with 'horizontal' information systems (see Figure 3.2).

Just as it makes sense to look at the different flows of information within an organisation, it makes sense to examine flows of information in systems that comprise a number of organisations. Thus, for the outsider, the systems of 'crime and punishment' are effectively homogeneous, a fact reflected in the term 'the criminal justice system'. To the professionals involved, there are in fact several independent organisations and several distinct systems: the police, the crown prosecution service, the defence lawyers, the judiciary and court systems, and the probation service. Within each of these vertical organisational 'silos', information will flow up and down. In contrast, horizontal flows between

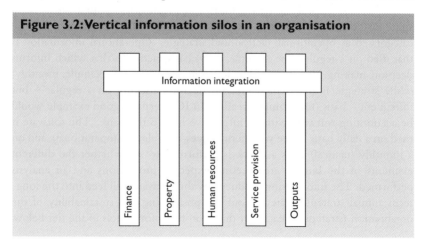

Figure 3.2: Vertical information silos in an organisation

Information integration

Finance

Property

Human resources

Service provision

Outputs

Figure 3.3: Vertical information silos in the criminal justice system

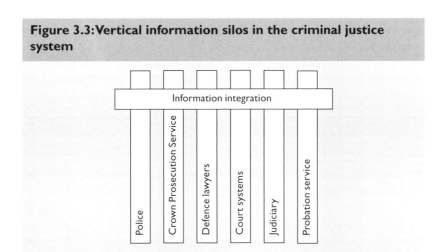

the silos may lead to problems and delays in decision making. Thus the UK's Coordination of Computerisation in the Criminal Justice System initiative seeks to enable information flows between criminal justice agencies, including the courts, prisons, police and probation service (Heeks, 1999, p 50) (see Figure 3.3).

If it is accepted that, for effective working, information has to flow appropriately both up and down and between organisations, it is not too hard to argue that to secure information integration within a team is easier than to ensure information integration within the department. In turn, this is easier than information integration within the organisation, which is itself easier than achieving information integration between organisations. With each higher 'level', though, the potential benefits become significantly greater (see Figure 3.4). Detailed examples of attempts to integrate information within and between social welfare organisations will be explored in Chapter Five.

Figure 3.4: Hierarchies of information integration

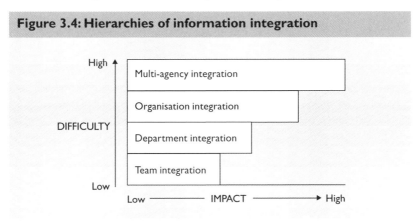

Just as individuals can take the view that new methods of managing information and greater collaboration around the sharing of information are problematic (whether because of anxieties about new technology, professional judgement or personal outlook), individuals through their professional status and organisational positions may resist new methods of managing information within or between organisations. Dutton (1996, p 270) list some 13 barriers, including:

- defence of functional boundaries by agency 'barons';
- constraints and demotivation faced by champions of innovation in the risk-averse bureaucratic cultures that typify many public agencies;.
- anxieties among staff caused by fears of employment cuts, job reorganisation and geographic redistribution;
- a perception among many staff and citizens that cost-cutting is the overriding objective ... and that claims about improving services fulfil a primarily rhetorical role.

At the Europe-wide level, Ducatel et al argues:

> ... public services and public administrations are vast repositories of information ... much of this potential is locked up because of unhelpful and rigid structures, departmental divisions, the constraints of bureaucratic procedures and even entrenched attitudes.... (Ducatel et al, 2000a, p 16)

The fact that so much knowledge resides in tacit and informal systems means that, even if the organisation is formally committed to new developments around information integration, delaying the process or even stopping it altogether may be a straightforward task. In that case, the barriers to integration are often less about technology and more about people.

Overblown claims for ICT don't help either. Since ICT can be only *one* part of the information management systems within and between organisations, most of the claims about the 'certain promises' of ICT are highly subjective and are subject to a wide range of conditions and circumstances. Furthermore, as was shown in Chapter One, these claims may in fact be further distorted by the objectives of those selling the ICT systems. The conditions and circumstances of success – and the cost of failure – are set out in Chapters Five and Six. But a realistic conclusion might be that ICT gives the potential for high reward – but at high risk (Audit Commission, 1994).

These three models – and the potential professional and organisational constraints – provide a basic lexicon with which to begin thinking about the information management systems of organisations – and it is these that Chapter Four will begin to address.

Thinklist

- **What knowledge does your work require you to have?**
- **Categorise this knowledge: is it tacit or explicit, informal or formal?**
- **Is this how it should be?**

FOUR

Modelling information flows and needs: improving service quality

Introduction

> Technology is not a requirement of an information system. (Daniels, 1994, pp 32-3)

In Chapter Three, the concept of information as an *entity* and some basic models of envisaging information were introduced. Chapter Four is divided into six sections:

- examining the process of developing an information management strategy;
- exploring the design, implementation and outcomes of a multi-agency, information management strategy – based on a case study of family support;
- focusing on the roles of communities of interest, especially as mediated through the Internet. It will explore how such 'virtual' communities can be self-generating, supported or established in partnership;
- examining the priority of *content* over *channel*;
- proposing in the last two sections a model of content enrichment and link this to developing quality services.

Developing an information management strategy

An ICT strategy is subsidiary to, and dependent on, an information strategy.

A simple way of conceiving this premise is to say that an information management strategy is "a means of delivering information from one person to another", while ICT is the technical apparatus for conveying that information (Daniels, 1994, pp 32-3).

In Chapter Three, the distinction was made between *content* and *carrier*, and this distinction holds here: the information strategy deals with the *content*, the ICT is merely the *carrier* of (or the channel for) the content.

Some key principles for an information strategy in an organisation are as follows (Abell and Oxbrow, 2001, p 242):

- Information is a corporate resource to be made available to all those who require it in order to perform their duties.
- Since information should be made available to complement decision making, the timeliness (and accuracy) of information is critical to its usefulness.
- The acquisition and maintenance of information resources represent a cost to the organisation that must be justifiable.
- Information must be acquired, processed and managed in a planned, integrated and economical way.

A helpful place to start in considering how to shape an information strategy is with the three 'S's: service users, staff, stakeholders.

- *Service users:* those citizens the organisation is working for and with. Depending on the agency and the setting, they may also be collectively known as the clients, the patients, the public, the users, the residents or the tenants.
- *Staff:* those who work for the organisation, the employees, and sometimes including volunteers. It also includes those who have a strategic role in, and statutory basis for, determining the direction of the organisation – for example, local authority councillors, board members and charity trustees.
- *Stakeholders:* these can include funders, including the taxpayer; elected representatives of the public (Members of Parliaments, Assembly Members, local councillors); general and specific regulators, such as health and safety agencies, the Charity Commission and inspection agencies; and groups representing service users.

Fundamental questions that an information strategy should answer are set out as a checklist in Box 4.1.

Since the precise make-up of service users, staff and stakeholders will vary between organisations, how information is gathered, managed, stored, retrieved and transmitted will vary too.

If these questions cannot readily be answered, there is no substitute for sitting down with the appropriate colleagues and attempting to map the current organisational – or departmental or team – situation. Information mapping is an essential precursor to any work being undertaken around ICT systems. It is the authors' experience that, in undertaking this exercise, one or two factors often emerge.

First, information maps, perhaps by another name, are often in place. For example, the organisation may have a human resources strategy that includes both employee records and systems for communicating with staff. The organisation may have a public relations programme for liaison with external stakeholders. If this is the case, so much the better; significant parts of the information map are already in existence.

Second, existing models of gathering, managing, storing, retrieving and transmitting information can be improved. Kerslake (1996, p 40) identifies a number of potential pitfalls here:

- Required information is collected and could be useful, but there is a low quality of collection and hence partial or incomplete sets of data are produced.
- Managers are not aware of the availability of data that can usefully be collected.
- Information is collated and presented in a format that cannot readily be understood or used.
- Information is collected which no one uses, yet the process of collection has become so entrenched in the organisation that it is hard to stop.
- Good information systems in an area may be abandoned at the expense of computerisation across a whole department or organisation.

Several of these points can be illustrated by a report on inspections by the Social Services Inspectorate, 'Management and use of information in social care' in eight English councils in 2002-03. "We saw efforts where the purpose of managing information had been lost, and information was being collected

---

Box 4.1: The fundamental questions of an information strategy

In meeting organisational objectives:
What do the three 'S's (service users, staff, stakeholders) need to know?
When do they need to know it?
In what form do they need to know it?

In gathering information:
Where does this information come from?
In what format?
What gaps are there?

In storing and retrieving this information:
How should this information be held?
Can it be accessed effectively?
Is it safe and secure?

In managing this information:
What work needs to be done, and by whom, in order to ensure that the information is current and accurate?

In transmitting the information:
Who does the information need to go to (service users, staff, stakeholders)?
In what format?
When and how often?

but not used". When one council did monitor the ethnicity of service users, the data were not compared with the make-up of the local population "so new knowledge was created and no decisions made on the basis of that knowledge" (DoH/SSI, 2003, p 40).

Once the information map is complete, an information strategy can take shape. In developing the information management strategy, a useful model has been produced by Earl, which he calls "information strategy formulation: a multiple methodology" (Earl, 1989, p 71). He contends that there are three main factors to take into account: 'top-down', 'bottom-up' and 'inside out'.

'Top-down' factors take into account issues such as objectives, overall working conditions, departments and organisations, leadership and vision. This can be caricatured as the 'where we'd like to be' approach. 'Bottom-up' encapsulates where the organisation is and what might be the next logical step. This is the 'where we are' approach. The 'inside out' element attempts to capitalise on the creative aspects of the organisation and existing models of an information strategy. Additionally, there are the elements of 'risk' (of failure) and 'speed' (of transformation) to be factored in. There will inevitably have to be some prioritisation reflecting what needs to be done first, by when and by whom (Earl, 1989). This process can be represented schematically in Figure 4.1.

A good example of a single-agency information management strategy is set out in Box 4.2 relating to small housing associations (SHAs). All three 'S's of staff, service users and stakeholders are considered.

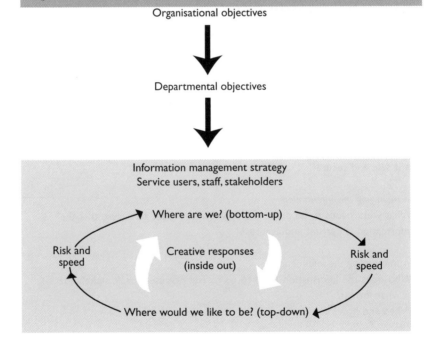

Figure 4.1: Developing an information management strategy

Organisational objectives

Departmental objectives

Information management strategy
Service users, staff, stakeholders

Where are we? (bottom-up)

Risk and speed

Creative responses (inside out)

Risk and speed

Where would we like to be? (top-down)

Box 4.2: Information management for small housing associations

This 'toolkit' for small housing associations (SHAs) is based on considering both internal and external information needs; whether the information systems needed should be computerised or not; and what controls are needed to ensure effective and efficient information management:

1. *Operational information*: key (usually computerised) databases are likely to be needed for day-to-day running of properties, tenants and finance, from which easy transfer of certain data to stakeholders (especially local authorities) can be provided.
2. *Control information*: the main control information compares financial performance with budget (again, usually computerised).
3. *Management information*: accurate information is needed to support managerial decision making through the analysis of day-to-day data and using internal criteria such as Key Performance Indicators or other standards.
4. *Communication information*: it is necessary to have readily accessible (ICT-maintained) information to communicate with staff and third parties, such as tenants and The Housing Corporation.
5. *Planning information*: in order to support future developments, information is needed to monitor the overall business strategy or plan, as well as for writing it in the first place. It should include internal performance information and benchmarking with other SHAs.
6. *External information*: each external stakeholder requires information relevant to them for partnership working (for example, local authorities) or regulatory bodies (for example, The Housing Corporation).

Source: adapted from National Housing Federation et al (2003, pp 10-12, Appendix A)

In this case study, the information-mapping exercise has produced six areas of attention: operational control, control information, management information, communication information, planning information and external information. Four clear strengths of this example can be identified:

- brevity – which does not preclude further detail in subsequent documents;
- a direct link to the organisational and departmental objectives;
- clarity, so that each staff member could, conceivably, be able to relate his or her work to the six areas; and
- usability, as an aide-memoire for the chief executive and departmental heads (area two for finance, area three for middle managers), as well as acting as a checklist for front-line staff.

A more detailed multi-agency example of information mapping and of development, implementation and review of an information management strategy is set out in the following section, through a case study of family support.

Prevention through communication

Origins and concept

'Prevention through Communication' was a family support strategy developed in the context of the so-called 'refocusing debate' in children and families services work from the mid-1990s. The national concern was that children in need were viewed as a low priority by welfare agencies and that there was no strategic view of family support services locally (DoH, 1995).

In addition, inspections had found that in many local authority areas there was no strategy for making information available about family support services and promoting it to service users and among agencies (SSI, 1997). Surveys also showed that "parents wanted to be treated in a non-stigmatised way by mainstream services, rather than be the targeted object of intervention" (Sinclair et al, 1997, p 25).

In practice, it was an approach to planning and delivering services to children and families though a *hierarchy of strategic information needs*. The location was an urban borough in the UK, with a number of very deprived wards and a large and diverse minority ethnic population.

In this strategy, a broad definition of family support was adopted, namely, that 'jigsaw' of agencies, professionals and resources which offers 'any activity or facility aimed at providing advice and support to parents to help them in bringing up their children' (Audit Commission, 1994).

Objectives

The strategy aimed to set up a number of routes whereby parents and children and young people could better self-access social welfare information. Equally important was the development of improved communication links between professionals and practitioners across agencies, so that they could provide quicker and more comprehensive information on current available services and refer families to the 'right' service where face-to-face support was needed.

Underpinning the operation of the strategy was the principle that communication and information needs must flow from the tasks of social welfare services, whether the provision of parenting support, public health improvement or reducing youth crime.

'First Contact'

In preparation for the strategy, the notion of 'First Contact – how children and families access information on services' was introduced to councillors and senior managers in social services, education, health, police, probation and the voluntary sector.

'First Contact' was defined as the initial enquiry to the council – or partner agency – which may, or may not, result in direct contact with a member of staff. Three main initial contact points for families in obtaining information on services are:

- self-access by parents, carers and young people;
- directly from professionals; and
- via the local authority's or other statutory agencies' customer services receptions.

Access to social welfare information on services tends to be through contact between the service user and the individual practitioner or professional delivering the service: for example, between social worker and family, GP and patient, child and teacher. Yet, on a particular issue, how does the service user know whom to approach in the first instance?

This provided a context for describing how the provision of information is, *in itself*, a service (see Chapter Three), alongside national trends and local developments towards increasing access to the Internet and ICT on the part of borough residents.

A triangle of family support needs and services

The key operating principle of the triangle is: the greater the need, the smaller the number of children (see Figure 4.2). Accordingly, at the apex of the triangle, services are likely to require the highest level of face-to-face intervention, rapid delivery, and be of the longest duration. By contrast, the largest number of children and families will be found at the base of the triangle, where many low-tier needs can be met by universal services, and printed and online information made available for self-access. At the intermediate tier of need, services including local or national telephone lines or a library book or video on a specialist area of child development would bridge the gap between the lowest need for information – via informal, open access support – and a greater need for formal structured interventions by professionals.

Underpinning the strategy is the recognition that families' needs vary in intensity, with intervention at low levels of need important too, and that the priorities of professionals may not be the priorities of parents and children. The corollary of accepting such principles is that, at the low and intermediate levels of need, the emphasis should be on enabling the potential service users to access information resources as and when they need them.

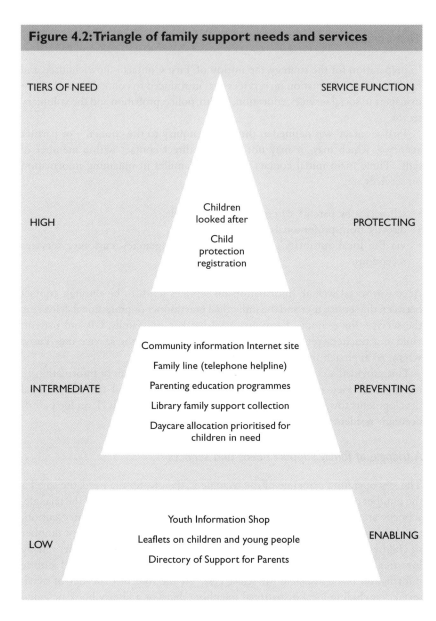

Figure 4.2: Triangle of family support needs and services

TIERS OF NEED   SERVICE FUNCTION

HIGH

Children
looked after

Child
protection
registration

PROTECTING

Community information Internet site

Family line (telephone helpline)

INTERMEDIATE   Parenting education programmes   PREVENTING

Library family support collection

Daycare allocation prioritised for
children in need

Youth Information Shop

Leaflets on children and young people

LOW   Directory of Support for Parents   ENABLING

Finally, services in the triangle include information (low need) as one type of service alongside types involving direct contact by telephone-line (intermediate need) or face-to-face contact with a practitioner or professional (high need).

Families may need to use services in more than one tier simultaneously. A family being supported on a casework basis (high need) by a statutory agency can also be using a telephone-line service for information on childcare (intermediate need) or accessing information on bullying (low need) in printed or electronic form via a library or 'one-stop shop'. Over time, for example, a bullying problem (low need) may escalate and advice from a specialist or parenting telephone-line service may be sought (intermediate need). Ultimately, in fewer cases, the impact on the child could result in referral for child and adolescent mental health services (high need).

Examples of service response to low, intermediate and high needs

At the low tier of need, dedicated children and young people racks of printed materials – giving local and national information on children's rights and services for children and their families – were set up in council libraries and one-stop shops. This reflected local MORI survey data showing that 55% of borough residents used libraries and 17% one-stop shops.

At the intermediate tier of need, 'FamilyLine' was a telephone service run by the Family Welfare Association (with Department of Health funding), which allowed families, in the evenings and at weekends, to access information about children's services in the borough. It provided an out-of-hours service to complement the role of the borough's one-stop shops in offering a front-line information and initial referral service.

Finally, the most face-to-face service work with children and families would take place at the high need part of the triangle. Within different agencies, this included child protection, tertiary health services from child psychiatric services and young people with truancy or behaviour problems being supported by education welfare officers.

The 'four-way flow'

Different agencies were asked to envisage what became known as the 'four-way flow'. Ultimately, the objective was for all children and families to move down the hierarchy of need: away from the tier of 'high need' and statutory intervention around child protection, and into the intermediate- or low-need tiers of family support. Conversely, agencies would seek to stop children and families moving up the hierarchy, by planning various types of early support. It was also recognised that families would often need different services within a tier of need and to be referred directly to agencies best placed to meet their needs – or 'signposted' to information resources – in a flow from side to side.

In Figure 4.3, these multi-directional 'flows' (represented as arrows) are transposed onto the triangle of family support needs, and reveal the dynamics of the 'Prevention through Communication' strategy.

Tools and processes

In this model, five agencies – social services, police, local education authority, health services and several voluntary sector services – were able to start from a point of agreeing common objectives (in this case family support); map the

Figure 4.3: Four-way flow

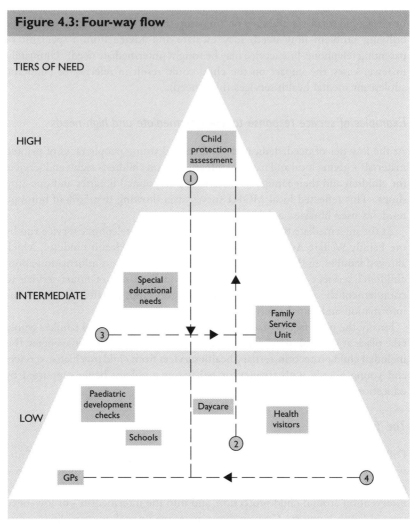

TIERS OF NEED

HIGH

INTERMEDIATE

LOW

Child protection assessment ①

Special educational needs

Family Service Unit

③

Paediatric development checks

Daycare

Health visitors

Schools

②

GPs ④

① A referral to children's social work from a school is decided by the duty team to be in the children in need, not child protection, category. The family is referred 'downwards' to information on bullying in the library family support collection and on the children and young people one-stop shop racks.

② A child protection referral from a neighbour is referred 'upwards' via the police to children's social work. Following a child protection investigation, conference and registration, danger of significant harm results in the child being looked after.

③ At a parenting class, families are introduced to resources of family support that exist in the intermediate tier, for example, the services at the Family Service Unit.

④ A health visitor uses a directory of support for parents as a reference tool to direct families to appropriate local or national statutory or voluntary organisations.

services provided in a comprehensive graphic (the hierarchy of needs); and identify how they could benefit from an information strategy. These corresponded with the start of the information management strategy (IMS) process – identifying organisational objectives. The use of 'one stop shops' was an inspired joint realisation to utilise existing facilities to promote family support (capitalising on Earl's 'inside out' element).

Due recognition needed to be given, in such processes, to understanding a little of the different terminology and culture across agencies, in order to embrace and not alienate different professional concerns and issues (see Chapter One).

Evaluation and outcomes

Evaluation was undertaken in various forums – for example, the Area Child Protection Committee and Early Years Development [and Childcare] Partnership – reflecting the multi-agency ownership of the strategy. Specific evaluation was possible, too, for particular agencies. For example, the local education authority could demonstrate how parts of the strategy contributed towards its core objective of improving schools and children's educational potential. For families, the children and young people racks served approximately 30,000 families across the borough with printed materials – with 12,500 leaflets taken in the first five months alone.

The project 'Prevention through Communication' was set up before the Internet became widely used, but it was integrated with increasing use of online information via local authority and community websites. Ultimately, sustainability was to be promoted through a cross-agency network of information 'champions' (at individual level) and by seeking synergies with new area-based initiatives, such as health action zones (at organisational level). However, the strategy was not developed further and its benefits were dissipated because of a loss of 'product champions' in the key agencies.

Communities of interest

In Chapter One, it was shown how, traditionally, communities have been linked to geographical space. Communities of interest – defined here as groups of individuals with particular characteristics, or a common cause, or economic interests, that transcend physical place – have always existed. They were mediated initially by letter and, increasingly throughout the 20th century, by phone. Currently, the development of the Internet has helped to broaden the range of such communities and increase the numbers of people participating. (For a comprehensive overview, see Pleace et al, 2003.)

In similar vein, groups have always come together to offer each other support and advice, and subsequently gone on to develop services. Nevertheless, ICT is effecting a transformation in this self-help and advocacy model. E-mail, chat rooms and message boards allow people to communicate not only with the service but with each other, so that "those people might never meet in person, but online they can share experiences and offer mutual support" (van Vark, 2003, p 18).

Four categories of 'virtual community' can be identified:

- those that arise through the development of new self-help groups (see *Pupiline*, Box 4.3);
- those that have come into existence in parallel with the development of the Internet;
- those that are a natural outgrowth of existing support and development work initiated by the voluntary sector (see *There4me* later in this chapter); and
- those that result from partnerships between e-government initiatives and the voluntary sector (see CareZone, later in this chapter).

The case of mental health

Communities of interest for people with mental health needs – adults and children – provide an illustration of the benefits of using ICT to develop 'virtual communities'.

There can be a stigma associated with mental health that may prevent people from accessing face-to-face services for professional help, let alone picking up a leaflet. The anonymity of accessing mental health information and guidance via the Internet can, therefore, ensure that a 'first contact' with social welfare support is taken up. Indeed, the interactivity of the technology can further promote access to support through the medium of 'online counselling'. This contains dimensions of non-stigmatising, self-access as well as direct professional intervention as group members can communicate with each other under the supervision of a health professional without having to be in the same physical place and at the same time. This ICT, self-access route is likely to be taken up more by young men with suicidal feelings than, say, older people experiencing schizophrenia (Hughes et al, 2002, p 91).

Bullying is a prevalent problem for children and young people, yet there can often be a stigma, accentuated by peer pressure, attached to seeking support from parents and teachers. In terms of the triangle of family support needs and services case study, at the lowest level of need a factual leaflet on bullying, made available in schools or via a website, is appropriate before the onset of more serious problems. When a child is being bullied, access to an interactive online website offering guidance and counselling may be most appropriate at this intermediate level of need. Only at the highest level of need – say, a child witnessing domestic violence – will face-to-face contact necessarily be required, perhaps via telephone line initially, to be followed by direct support with a relevant professional.

Box 4.3 shows an online 'virtual community' of interest and support for children and young people (*Pupiline*).

Box 4.3: *Pupiline*

Pupiline is a peer-based website, started up in 2000 by a 15-year-old as a peer forum for teenagers to talk about bullying. It began when Oli Watts (Managing Director, Pupiline Ltd) simply posted his story of being bullied on the Internet to seek peer support in the absence of any 'friendly' information that he could find on the web to help him. The main pages are Features, Issues and Advice, Forums and Local Areas. Forum subjects range from teenage pregnancy to exam stress, but the forum that receives the most visitors is the one on bullying. Advice includes how to prepare for exams to reduce stress and what to do and what not to do when bullied, along with information on children's rights ('your school must do certain things to protect you from bullying'). The site, with all contributors under 21, emphasises that *Pupiline* is not offering professional advice, so the website provides hypertext links to organisations that do. It works with local and central authorities, support agencies and commercial organisations. *Pupiline's* philosophy of ... *for us by us©* has been recognised by many awards.

Sources: Southam (2001, p 10); Watts (2002); www.pupiline.net

Content is king

Making information accessible

Writing for social welfare clients, in whichever field, is "about communicating with people. It's about helping people understand" (Hopkins, 1998, p 20). The point was made earlier in this chapter that there is a fundamental difference between *content* and *channel*. The issue of content now merits further analysis and comment.

Printed leaflets and websites must be readable and easy to use so that the content being communicated is accessible – but jargon is regularly cited as a major problem. Sadly, one does not have to look too far in the public and voluntary sectors to see information that fails to meet this basic criterion.

In the UK, the pressure group, the Plain English Campaign (www.plainenglish.co.uk) has been at the forefront of promoting to public, voluntary and private sector organisations the benefits of clarity in written communication. Its 'Crystal Mark' has become well established as the standard that all organisations should aim for when they produce public information. This is awarded on the basis of technical tests and only after independent testing on the public.

A common problem is agencies taking badly written printed literature and then loading it onto their websites, often heralding this as a breakthrough in improving access to and communication with their clients. This may signal a confusion of content with carrier, the assumption being that since the carrier is 'cutting-edge' the content must be too. Specific problems of content frequently revolve around the following:

- *Use of jargon:* the dangers of jargon were raised in Chapter One. While it can be 'a useful shorthand that enables prompt, clear and concise communication between those [professionals] who understand it', too often it is "used to impress, exclude or is just used unthinkingly" (Hopkins, 1998, pp 72-3).
- *Writing for the wrong audience:* all too often local government officers seem to be writing for other local government officers (rather than service users and council taxpayers). Similarly, civil servants draft papers reflecting the syntax of their current ('New Labour') ministers.
- *Lack of clarity about the function of the communication effort:* this can be seen in the voluntary sector, where there are still too many 'brochure' sites. Writing for such websites represents a particular challenge, since individuals may visit the site from a range of agencies – funders, service users, trustees and potential volunteers. (For a good guide to communication issues, see Harrison, 1995.)

Again, the distinction between channel and content is instructive. The skills and techniques (channels) for putting together a TV item and a newspaper article are different, even if both channels are covering the same story (content). It is better to acknowledge that the mediums provided by ICT need to be used in specific ways and in specific circumstances (see Chapter Three). The technology of ICT produces particular problems and constraints (see Box 4.4).

Box 4.4: Making a web page usable

Jacob Nielsen's text 'New riders' (www.useit.com) is a web design classic, having sold over a quarter of a million copies in 21 languages. Among his views are the following:

- People read 25% more slowly from PC monitors than from the page, so write succinctly.
- Miss out slow-loading graphics wherever possible, especially when they add no value to the text. Otherwise users will become bored and surf elsewhere on the net.
- The web designer does not control the way the page is seen; depending on computer set-up, page elements including sizes and colours may appear in different ways from those expected.
- Develop a clear site structure so that at each stage users can see where they are in the overall website.

Source: Wilson (2002)

In order to promote 'usability', the Plain English Campaign also offers a so-called Internet Crystal Mark logo to show a commitment to plain English throughout a website. Assessment criteria cover not only the text but also navigation devices, page design, use of colour and so forth. At the time of writing, 65% of the members of the Internet Crystal Mark scheme were social welfare or public service agencies.

A second aspect of 'usability' is the accessibility of the website along the dimensions of culture, language, gender, ethnicity and disability. These issues will be addressed in detail in Chapter Seven, as issues central to the 'digital divide'.

Finally, an innovative example of a website where content and interactivity are prominent is CareZone (www.thewhocarestrust.org.uk). As well as universal websites for children and young people (see Chapter Seven, for example www.thesite.org), there is also a key role to be played by specialist sites for particularly vulnerable or disadvantaged groups.

E-mail, chat rooms and message boards

"Self-help networks of people sharing advice and information are ... being stimulated by the internet." While the number of self-help groups – whether Alcoholics Anonymous or reading groups – "was already growing before the internet ... electronic communications often supplement existing networks" (Jupp and Bentley, 2001, p 102). In this section, this phenomenon will be outlined through use of e-mail, message boards and chat rooms.

E-mail (electronic mail) is a way of sending messages and text files from one computer to another via the Internet. The first e-mail was sent in 1971; today, an estimated 10 billion e-mails are sent globally each day. To send and receive e-mail, a person must have an e-mail address and a mailbox on a server computer. E-mails are basic text files, but they can also carry Word files, spreadsheets and graphics, for example, as attachments (Hughes et al, 2002, p 15).

A message board (or forum) provides a method by which individuals accessing a website can post messages to a publicly accessible online 'notice board' in a process similar to e-mail. An initial posting on a message board will create a new topic or subject for consideration. Responses to the message can be posted and, after a series of responses, a 'conversation tree' can develop. Message boards provide users with the opportunity to ask questions, voice opinions, debate issues, provide information, or make public announcements on issues of mutual interest. It is normal to require people to register with the host site in order to post replies to topics, but most boards are viewable by anyone without the need to register. Message boards can therefore create an archive of user interaction that in itself is a content-rich resource. For example, a search of a message board dealing with technical ICT problems might throw up information without the user having to create a new topic and wait for a useful reply.

Rather than creating a board on which to post messages, a chat room offers the possibility of user interaction of a different nature. It creates a space that users must log into. In order to log in, a site visitor must pick a 'username' (not necessarily a real name). Visitors are then able to see a list of the other people logged in at the same site, under the same subject, at the same time, thereby creating a 'virtual room' in which people can 'see' each other. A user can then type in a message through his or her web browser, which, once sent, all the users in the room will be able to read and respond to as they wish. Unlike a message board or e-mail, the interaction is live (synchronous) or more or less 'real time'. Transcripts of chat room interactions are not commonly saved. In advocacy and community development terms (see Chapter Two), the chat room may constitute a forum in which a small group of people engage in a rapid exchange of ideas and experiences and foster a sense of (virtual) community between participants (Safer Internet, 2003g).

Some key guidance for setting up message boards and chat rooms is set out in Box 4.5.

A strong self-help element lies at the centre of a young people-led initiative to support isolated young people who have experienced bereavement (see Box 4.6).

When one develops a chat room, it is also necessary to be aware that it can pose a particular danger to children and young people. This is because chat rooms are easily accessible and there is no way of verifying the identity of the person a child is talking to (see Internet safety discussion in Chapter Two). Good principles of web-based counselling and advice services (Loga, 2003) include:

- police checks on all staff;
- supervision and support from trained counsellors;

Box 4.5: Message boards and chat rooms

- The aim should be to allow people to exchange views and win peer support as well as gain some insight into the organisation's aims and the support it can offer.
- A chat room may be harder to maintain as, unlike a message board, it is a 'live' forum and needs users in it at the same time to work.
- A monitoring role – through an 'active moderator' – is essential both to manage risk (for example, libellous postings, for which liability may rest with the website owner) and activity (for example, may need to answer questions or catalyse discussion if quiet).
- "It's better to have no chat room than to have an empty one".

Source: van Vark (2003)

- encryption of chat and e-mail to prevent hackers accessing personal details; and
- advice on ensuring that other users of the same computer cannot see which sites have been used.

There4me.com is a highly interactive NSPCC website, of which offers information, advice and counselling on a broad range of issues to young people aged 12-16. The security of the website is paramount, to guard against unauthorised access to 'real-time' online counselling and to its message board and chatroom features (www.there4me.com).

The field of parenting advice has also been changed with the advent of Internet chat rooms within parenting websites. The social support available enables parents – in particular, mothers – to "return to the most traditional source of support of all: other mothers". This model works well for parents in "isolated communities" and where there is "a specific diagnosis or issue" (Moorhead, 2003).

The content enrichment model

A number of authorities have begun to make the distinction between 'standard' websites and 'transactional' websites. Standard websites offer little more than the information that a piece of paper can display, whereas transactional websites offer a range of services to users. For example, in the private sector there are currency calculators for frequent travellers (see, for example, www.economist.com or www.ft.com/calculators); in the public sector it is possible to complete your tax return online and have your return calculated (www.inlandrevenue.gov.uk).

Martin Greenwood (2003) of the Society of Information Technology Managers (SOCITM) offers a spectrum of websites in which the transactional site is the most highly developed:

Box 4.6: Youth involvement project website

A major part of a Cruise Bereavement Care project has been a website developed specifically for young people experiencing bereavement and loss. Services include general advice and information, a message board on which young people can talk about their situation and about how to access professional support. Based on a peer support model, a group of young volunteers (aged 16-25) answer e-mails sent in confidence to the site, including messages divulging self-harming behaviour. Young people can also gain support in developing friendship networks.

Sources: Slater (2003, pp 24-5); www.rd4u.org.uk

- no website
- promotional website
- content
- content plus
- transactional.

Similarly, Saxton and Game (2001) distinguish between voluntary sector sites that simply offer information and those that facilitate interaction by entering a chat room, donating, campaigning (for example, signing an e-petition), purchasing (say, charity Christmas cards) and so forth.

However, a third and higher category of website is beginning to emerge – a site that no longer passively responds to the user but takes the initiative. A good example of this is www.tfl.gov.uk/journey. By registering at this Transport for London website, users automatically receive an e-mail or text message informing them of any delays or problems with the trains, buses or tubes on their normal commute.

Three hierarchies can thus be identified: inform, interact and initiate. *Interact* provides higher content enrichment than *inform*, and, in turn, *initiate* provides higher content enrichment than *interact* (see Figure 4.4).

However, websites should not remain isolated from other forms of content. A telling example of such isolation is the frequent failure of organisations to promote their websites. Saxton and Game (2001) found that voluntary sector organisations frequently missed such opportunities. Website addresses should be on annual reports, letterheads, business cards, and in e-mail signatures (the 'sign-off' text that can be automatically added at the end of every message).

The content on the website is thus supplementary not 'substitutionary' to the provision of other forms of content and exchange, like printed material, face-to-face contact and telephone lines. This is reflected in UK e-government policy (see Chapter Eight). The Prime Minister envisaged that:

> ... the Internet, interactive TV and touchscreen delivery should take their place alongside more innovative use of the telephone, the call centre and the paper document, not replace them; nor should face-to-face contact be replaced where that is what is needed. (Prime Minister and Minister for the Cabinet Office, 1999)

Service quality and integrated information management

Defining service quality in information management

How can service quality be improved through information management?

> In direct terms, improved delivery to social welfare clients can be enabled through staff being better informed about their needs and up to date with

Figure 4.4: Content enrichment

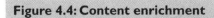

LOW   CONTENT ENRICHMENT   HIGH

Inform	Interact	Initiate

ACTIVITY	ACTIVITY	ACTIVITY
• Read • Look at graphics For example • Myriad websites	• Chat rooms • Purchase • Donate • Campaign (for example, via e-mail) • Support For example • Submit claims • Calculate claims	• Proactive service provision For example • Text/e-mail/SMS travel alerts www.tfl.gov.uk/ journey

professional and service developments in the field. Enhanced provision of information can be a service improvement in itself. Indirectly, information management will support the production of better strategic policies or operational plans, leading to more positive outcomes for service users. (Ticher and Powell, 2000, p 27)

A key element in ensuring the effectiveness of an information management strategy is to develop and implement it through a service quality model (for example, 'total quality management'). In overall terms, quality assurance within an organisation means that "the organisation should be expected to perform consistently to set standards of good practice. The standards act as minimum guarantees that users and producers can expect from the organisation" (Lawrie, 1995, p 68).

In order to build quality assurance into the information management process, stages of clarification, learning, standard setting, development and review should be introduced. These are set out in Box 4.7.

Box 4.7: Quality assurance in the information management process

Clarification	*Is the organisation clear about the information it needs?* If the organisation does not need the information, staff should not be asked to produce it. This is linked to having identified the intended service users as well as considering the needs of staff and other stakeholders.
Learning	*How do we ensure the 'right' content?* This requires both creating a continual process of learning from users, as well as identifying good practice within the organisation.
Standard setting	*'Who' should know 'what' information 'when'?* Quality standards need to be clear, specific, measurable and attainable (in that the organisation must have resources to meet the standard). Do staff know who is responsible for what?
Development	Is information comprehensively managed? Gaps between current practice and intended quality standards need to be identified and action taken to 'plug' them. Also, is there evidence of duplication or of areas where information collected for one purpose can be used for another (economies of scale)?
Review	*Have the parameters of information management changed over time?* Does the organisation have new information needs that are not currently being met? Service users, staff and stakeholders need to be involved in reviewing and monitoring the standards to reflect their changing expectations.

Sources: adapted from Lawrie (1995, pp 69-76); Ticher and Powell (2000, pp 20, 29)

A crucial and direct contribution to service quality will be provided, too, through field practice. In turn, this is increasingly supported via e-learning, such as ICT training for teachers and computerised diagnostic software for primary healthcare staff in NHS Direct. In this way, information management skills and continuous professional development are integrated to improve front-line practice. As a new study on *Redefining work 2* asserts, "technology democratises knowledge, by enabling more people within organisations to share it; so people are no longer as good as their knowledge, but as good as their ability to process it" (Bayliss, 2003, p 7).

This chapter has set out how to establish an information management strategy and its ICT strategy. The ICT strategy is part of the wider whole, and must therefore fall entirely within the information management strategy. This can be summarised by the key principle of integrated information management in Figure 4.5.

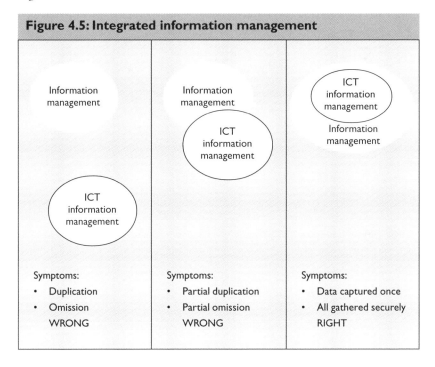

Figure 4.5: Integrated information management

Chapter Four has also differentiated the key concepts of content and channel and – through a content enrichment model – information management links with service quality issues were outlined. Chapter Five goes on to explore the specifics of an ICT strategy. ICT developments will be related to theories of organisational and service development in order to demonstrate the impact of information management on improving service quality for social welfare users.

Thinklist

- **What are your main flows of information?**
- **Do you have an information management strategy?**
- **What might this mean for the three 'C's: content, channel, communication?**

FIVE

Modelling information flows and needs: improving organisational effectiveness

Introduction

In Chapter Four, the building blocks of integrated information management were outlined, including the relationship between ICT and non-ICT information management. This chapter will:

- emphasise the importance of *channel* in relation to *content*, and underline how ICT is supplementary to other channels;
- introduce the importance of the 'value chain' in information management; and
- highlight three areas of attention with regard to information integration: *within* the organisation, *between* organisations, and *over* organisations.

This chapter will aim to show how integrated and cross-agency perspectives of inter-organisational information management can improve social welfare outcomes.

Information management and appropriate channels

Information needs of service users

Any information management strategy needs to 'flow' from the function and tasks of the social welfare organisation. In turn, this is determined by the organisational objectives, professional perspectives and the needs (and views) of users. As was explained in Chapter Four, communication is an integral element of the information management strategy.

In the process of communication the choice of channel is critical. If, for example, the welfare issue to be communicated is about current housing legislation and homelessness, there will be a number of channels available to reach a number of audiences. The sequence may consist of:

- the development of general material around housing and homelessness (*content*);

- the broadcasting of this material to particular audiences via specific mechanisms, like a leaflet or poster (*channel*);
- the development of audience-specific material; for example, it may be desirable to produce specific material for the needs of young people who are, or are at risk of becoming, homeless (*content*). This material may need to be broadcast via specific channels, such as youth magazines and websites (*channel*). Other audience-specific material (*content*) will need to be developed for partner agencies to ensure coordinated service provision (*channel*);
- the further development of distinct channels for distinct user groups, including minority ethnic languages, Braille and audiotape to maximise accessibility. (For a fuller discussion of these principles and application, see Harrison, 1995.)

Different channels have distinct strengths and weaknesses. It is a mistake to assume that one form of channel automatically has primacy over another – for example, that the printed word has primacy over the electronic word or vice versa. Indeed, the electronic word can have very specific problems (see Chapter Seven).

For groups that require face-to-face support, front-line professionals will continue to play a key role. Telephone contact will also continue to fulfil a major role. ICT systems can *supplement* these tried and tested mechanisms, but they cannot *substitute* for them. A good example of this is NHS Direct (see Chapter One). The channels that NHS Direct provides enhance, but do not replace, the fundamental relationship between the professional or practitioner and the patient.

ICT does have a major advantage in that content can easily be modified for different channels. Thus, video footage produced on a digital video camera:

- can be edited and re-edited for various audiences quickly and simply by using affordable software;
- can be applied easily to a wide range of channels, including CD ROM, DVD, the web, e-mail or VHS video;
- can have digital effects (for example, on-screen captions) easily applied via software;
- can then be disseminated via television, with, for example, some charities pioneering a sophisticated tool of 'advertiser-funded' or 'branded' programming.

Digitised material can be searched, recombined and linked to provide greater accessibility, flexibility and integration, for the benefit of the service user (see Box 5.1).

The remainder of this chapter will consider the theory and practice of how organisations model information flows and thereby improve their effectiveness.

Box 5.1: British Heart Foundation

The British Heart Foundation produced a 'Heartland' series, working with a production company, *twofourtv*. It is a 12-part magazine-format show that incorporates important messages about heart disease. With material originally developed for use in the Foundation's education videos, the aim is to produce an entertaining show that manages to reinforce the key health promotion messages of the charity. The series was shown on the cable Health Channel and also broadcast in some GP surgeries.

Source: Capeling (2002, p 55)

Added value and the information chain

Porter's concept of 'valued added'

For every organisation – whether private, public or voluntary – there are essentially four stages (see Figure 5.1).

These processes can be envisaged as a chain. Each link in the chain incurs cost and should add value. Therefore, in the private sector, companies will aim to reduce their costs with each link but to maximise the value – and hence profit – of the final item. (For a full discussion of the concept of the 'value chain', see Porter, 1998.)

Chapter One introduced the idea of the knowledge worker and the extent to which professionals and practitioners in social welfare embody this notion. In this model, the value chain can be seen not as a tangible material product (of inputs, activities and outputs), but as information that flows through and is used effectively by the organisation (Porter and Millar, 1998).

In Chapter Two, it was argued that information was a basic building block of social welfare work, and the management of this information was a precursor to making effective decisions and taking appropriate action. In the information chain model, each input is an information-gathering exercise and each output is an effective action. The task, then, is to ensure that there is no unnecessary duplication involved and that the information value is maximised.

Figure 5.1: Adding value

Inputs	Activity	Outputs	Outcomes

Source: adapted from Lawrie (1995, p 44)

Information chain analysis can show an organisation:

- what information it needs to obtain;
- where that information might come from; and
- how intra- or inter-organisational systems might improve their outputs (Edwards et al, 1995, p 61).

What is important to note at this stage is that the insertion of ICT into the information value chain will destabilise existing models. For example, the advent of word-processing software from the late 1980s has meant the demise of the role of typist. The realisation that ICT has the potential to streamline the process of information gathering, storage, manipulation and transmission has become the basis for new management models.

Analysing the information value chain can thus be a "valuable way of identifying where better information and systems are needed" (Edwards et al, 1995, pp 72-3). Some tools for undertaking this task will be introduced in Chapter Six. At this stage, however, the issue of how information chains that use ICT are being developed *within* organisations, *between* organisations and *over* organisations must be explained.

Within the organisation

The idea that the inputs of information chains could be condensed or simply eliminated led to such ideas as 'single-point information gathering' (see Box 5.2).

Box 5.2: Single-point information gathering

This idea is that in any large organisation, such as a local authority or NHS Trust, an individual's address may be held in multiple departments. So the details of a person with a disability may be recorded under council tax, parking permits, library, children's school, electoral roll and social services occupational therapy, as well as under the NHS physiotherapy department. Changes of address involve multiple phone calls, letters or e-mails, to be followed by the local authority and NHS repeating the same task over and over. In areas of high mobility, this proliferation of simple administrative tasks has the potential, at best, to consume significant resources. At worst, significant risks are created, say, when the families of children on the child protection register move and agencies in the new area are unaware of their presence. Ideally, ICT should capture an address change once, then automatically transmit it through linked agencies, and 'flag up' possible action needed (for example, when a child on the register leaves an area).

Between organisations

From organisational silos to inter-organisational integration

It is useful, first, to consider the ICT 'baseline' within social services and health agencies towards the end of the 1990s. As late as 1999-2000, government inspections of 10 social services departments in England found that, at the most basic level, "telecommunication systems were not adequate to carry the volume of traffic, and service users were unable to contact social workers". In addition, inspectors found it not surprising that "health authorities and trusts often used information technology which was incompatible with their neighbours and other agencies" (SSI, 2001, pp 12, 22).

In the development of ICT systems in the UK's public services, a laissez-faire approach has meant that information cannot flow seamlessly between these agencies and, therefore, "operational information silos" exist in health, education, police, housing, social services, probation, and so on (Milner, 2002, p 13). The current challenge is to integrate "cross-boundary operations, organisational structures, and information technology systems" so that ICT applications can become truly inter-organisational (Caldow, 2002, p 19; Milner, 2002, p 11).

It was estimated in 1997 that there were six different 'chains' across the whole public service delivery network, with 45,500 outlets. Since government departments did not develop their ICT in any form of a shared data network, different parts of the government machine – Inland Revenue, local authorities, NHS, Employment Service, public records office – have been operating "discrete information storage and processing systems" (Byrne, 1997, p 11). Few benefits from economies of scale or more coordinated service delivery could accrue.

Of course, an effective information chain may improve services yet not necessarily reduce the cost of delivery. In the case of the NHS Direct call-centre approach, the application of remote diagnosis – on the basis of computerised triage procedures – actually seems to have increased front-line referral rates to other parts of the NHS (Milner, 2002, pp 6-7). On the other hand, further ICT development of the electronic patient record, for example, could help to improve the service response to patients and yield cost efficiencies.

This can also be illustrated in the social care field, where a new requirement was announced by the UK government in 2002 for local authorities and partner agencies in England to develop information, referral and tracking (IRT) systems for all children. There will be significant development costs of audit, planning and implementation, but long-term cost benefits could result from improved preventive working by the agencies concerned and the avoidance of more costly later intervention (see Box 5.3).

Whether such schemes as IRT will succeed as planned is uncertain at the end of 2003. On the positive side, IT systems are being modernised in the NHS and criminal justice agencies to allow them to share such information. Yet a survey of 80 councils found that 85% of social services departments lack

Box 5.3: Information, referral and information systems

The original idea was for the main children's services agencies to better identify, assess and, where necessary, refer on every child 'at risk', and then be able to track that child's progress through, between and within agencies. The rationale is not to create whole new ICT systems, but to better integrate information systems across local agencies. This is to be based on 'information hubs' to be developed in every local authority. These shared electronic databases of all the children living in their area are to contain basic details, such as GP, school attended (or excluded from) and a 'flag' if known to one of the agencies. Under the information, referral and information (IRT) system, all professionals in relevant agencies will then be able to log their initial concerns on a shared system of procedures. Trailblazers involving 15 local authorities are piloting approaches during 2003-04. (See also Chapter Two for a discussion of confidentiality issues in IRT.)

Sources: HM Treasury (2002); NCVCCO (2002); Children and Young People's Unit (2002); Gillen (2003, p 8); DfES (2003, pp 52-3); Batty (2003, p 10); Cross (2003)

a database capable of monitoring contact with other welfare and criminal justice agencies; 8% felt that the task will take as long as five years (Headstar, 2003).

It may be more realistic to say that "the process of achieving an open operating environment [across public services] with high levels of connectivity is likely to be an evolutionary process" (Strassman, 1995, cited in Milner, 2002, p 11).

A final, key dimension of the information chain is the need in information management to put "information at the heart of every employee's work experience". This approach recognises that the recipients of information in the chain are not ciphers but key actors and "part of the knowledge process". There is a two-way requirement: the organisation's strategy needs to "take into account the culture and people aspects of information collection and sharing"; at the same time, "employees have a personal obligation to access information sources" (Abell and Oxbrow, 2001, pp 241-2; see also Chapter Two).

'Back office' to 'front office'

Put simply, the terms 'front office' and 'back office' are used to differentiate between those systems and processes that a client or customer sees, uses or interacts with ('front office' – for example, product ordering systems, customer services, or service information), and those the public does not see or interact with ('back office' – which includes all the systems that plan, resource, analyse and support product, service or information delivery). In short, 'front office' means customer-facing services, while 'back office' business processes and systems are needed in support (LondonConnects, 2001, pp 17-18). The ambition of transforming public services through ICT rests on the practical ways that improvements to the back office will, through the information chain, bring benefits to citizens at the front office.

Back office

For one organisation to link its back office ICT with another's, the following prerequisites must be satisfied:

• there is effective information management;
• operational systems are effective, with staff actively involved in customising ICT systems to their working practices; and
• operational systems are reliable, with data being kept complete, accurate and current.

As was shown in Chapter Three, data becomes information only when some meaning has been ascribed to it; and, as Henri Giller (1996, p 44) puts it, "the assumption that within or between agencies there is a shared frame of reference or understanding in making the data meaningful is frequently flawed". Box 5.4 offers a basic checklist – conceived by Ticher and Powell (2000) for use in the voluntary sector – to ensure that there is an understanding of what each organisation wants from the relationship and how each organisation works.

At the ICT back office, with the proper data safeguards, "information can flow seamlessly and invisibly across service boundaries" (Milner, 2002, p 2). This means that across public services collection of data can be streamlined, case communication between agencies improved, and front-line staff – in call centres and in initial referral or assessment roles – can have better access to accurate and comprehensive information (Prime Minister and Minister for the Cabinet Office, 1999). In these ways, back-office integration can help deliver

---

Box 5.4: Exchange of information between organisations

• Why is my organisation making the link?
• Why are the other parties involved making the link?
• What sort of information needs to be exchanged and why – in terms of content, quality and timeliness?
• Who is responsible for confidentiality and data protection policy?
• Is the level of commitment in terms of time and resources adequate for the purpose in hand and clear?
• Are the practical arrangements for the linkage appropriate to the responsibilities assigned to it and the amount of work involved?
• What are the procedures for breaking the link, should any party desire this?

Source: Ticher and Powell (2000, p 91)

---

significant improvements to the modernising (and 'joined-up') government agenda in healthcare, social care, education, benefits and personal taxation, and to citizens' involvement with the criminal justice system.

Indeed, the transition between a basic and a more complex back-office integration is now apparent in the UK, driven 'top-down' by e-government imperatives and developed through large-scale initiatives and smaller pilots. In the mid- and late 1990s, various 'extranet' initiatives were piloted at national and local levels. Essentially, if the intranet provides an Internet network that is secured for use within one organisation, an extranet, at its simplest, is the connection between two or more intranets to allow for collaboration on data-sharing and/or multi-agency operational processes.

Two UK examples of back-office integration are provided by social welfare services in the education and criminal justice systems respectively (in Boxes 5.5 and 5.6).

In the area of child protection, many tragic and high-profile cases in the UK (most recently, that of Victoria Climbié), in which children have 'fallen through the net' of social care services, have in common the contributory factor of poor inter-agency information sharing and communication (Secretary of State for Health et al, 2003). Box 5.7 describes an IRT pathfinder project in London and Liverpool to improve child protection information management across local health and social care services.

Front office

The ideal outcome of back-office integration supporting front-office delivery is that whether they go online directly or via a professional or customer services, users of social welfare or public services should experience the presentation of

---

Box 5.5: Pan-London Register for school admissions

This is a back-office to back-office project to improve the coordination of school admissions across London local education authorities (LEAs). When each LEA receives its applications from parents, those that are for schools in other boroughs will be uploaded to a central 'e-repository', the Pan-London Register (PLR). The receiving LEAs will then be able to download this information direct into their own local admissions systems (LASs). The PLR will not provide any allocation processing. The LAS will be the system that decides on the best offer for each pupil, although the PLR is used to transmit the decisions between each LAS. The idea is that people will receive only one offer of a secondary school place regardless of where in London they apply, and the project should help different LEAs systems to integrate. The project is being managed by Wandsworth LEA and is part-funded by the Office of the Deputy Prime Minister.

Sources: Arete Software Ltd (2003); correspondence with Brent LEA

Box 5.6: VISOR sex and violent offender database

A single, national database for England and Wales was developed from 2002 to meet the needs of the national probation and police services, in order to enable effective risk assessment, management and supervision of violent offenders, sex offenders and dangerous offenders through local Multi-Agency Public Protection Arrangements. The need arose from the limitations of local systems that generally do not operate across other police and probation areas, while offenders in these categories often travel across the agency boundaries. While having to comply with the Human Rights and Data Protection Acts, the system is designed as a tool for managing offenders, as well as being a powerful searchable resource for investigations of serious crimes. For example, VISOR will make it possible to search for descriptive details relating to personal data on offenders, including pictures of personal features and methods of operation.

Source: unpublished police and probation service papers

Box 5.7: Child Protection on Line project

In the Health Action Zone area of Lambeth, Southwark and Lewisham, Child Protection on Line (CPoL) was initiated in 2001 as a fast and secure system that allows NHS Accident and Emergency (A&E) nurses and clinicians to interrogate the Child Protection Registers (CPRs) of the three boroughs. The aim is to ensure that clinicians and social services professionals can communicate and share information more effectively to safeguard children at risk of abuse on a 24-hours-a-day basis. Health professionals can run a search from the combined CPR database of the social services departments; and the enquiry, along with the A&E episode number, name of the health professional and reason for search will be securely encrypted and e-mailed to the appropriate social services team(s). CPoL has been extended to participating social services and health authorities in Liverpool. It is a working 'hub and spoke' model of inter-agency information sharing and communication that should be adaptable for other uses. At the end of 2003, CPoL's lead sponsor and other partners were awaiting a decision on government sponsorship to extend electronic access to CPRs of all social services departments in London by authorised A&E clinicians across the capital's NHS Trusts.

Source: unpublished papers and presentations of the NHS South East London Shared Services Partnership

information and the process of making a transaction as if they were in communication with a single agency. This is an electronic equivalent of the one-stop shop (face-to-face) model.

A central motif of the current UK government is 'joined-up' government. This aims to integrate operational and policy responses to those social problems that cross traditional service boundaries. In the case of ICT, this is not merely metaphorical – government literally needs to be connected together by an ICT infrastructure:

> There is in embryo here a wholly new approach to the interaction between citizen and state, greatly facilitated by the IT revolution. It is replicated in the pioneering NHS Direct service. No longer will divisions within government organisations befuddle the citizen. One phone call, one visit, one Internet hit puts an integrated system to work. It is the ultimate challenge of joined up government. (Miliband, 1999, p 13)

As the range and level of interactivity for online social welfare services increase, citizens will have more opportunities to adopt a 'self-service' approach to making initial enquiries and conducting transactions. This should be to their greater convenience and to the government's reduced costs. Nevertheless, the back office still has some way to go before these front-office benefits can develop. A recent inspection of English social services departments found that "websites were, in general, a promotional rather than interactive channel, with limited opportunity for users and carers to be active in organising their own care..." (DoH, 2003, p 8).

While front-office developments for direct self-access by the public and service users are gradually progressing, the equivalent piloting of schemes is taking place where the ICT is at one remove from the citizen. In other words, social welfare professionals, in their direct practice with users, are able to access, use and transmit data at the front-office/back-office interface.

In the late 1990s, the UK government envisaged Internet-enabled laptop computers being used to support a housing officer, health visitor or community worker in outreach work so that they could operate similarly to, say, a fixed location one-stop shop (Cabinet Office, 2000). By the start of the 21st century, the portability factor meant that mobile phones and palmtop computers had come to be seen as more practical platforms. For example, during 2003, a number of children's social services departments in England and Wales were "developing or testing methods of portering information from a computer-based information system held on their central server computer to laptop or handheld computers that staff can carry with them on visits to clients and when away from the office". Such information 'portered' may include details about particular cases, tasks and contacts, and forms to be completed with client details, "ready to be uploaded to the central server on return to the office" (DoH and the Welsh Assembly Government, 2003, p 10).

Similarly, within a fixed setting – an emergency hospital in Germany – tablet PCs are being used like clipboards to record key information 'on the move' with improved speed and accuracy. A wireless local area network captures the data collected en route through Accident & Emergency (A&E) admission stages,

Box 5.8: New York Division of Parole

Parole officers in the New York State Division of Parole use a small hand-held ICT device in operational work in the field. They insert relevant information, which is then processed remotely. The data are subsequently accessible to the officers at their main workplace, at other agencies or in the field again, and are transmitted and stored in a safe and convenient way. A laptop platform would not have been practical, as the nature of the parole officer's role requires their hands to be free for security reasons.

Source: Caldow (2002, pp 34-5)

and both text and drawings written directly on to the hand-held screens are transferred onto the main computer systems (Microsoft, 2003). An international example, in the probation field, is drawn from the US (see Box 5.8).

'Wi-Fi' technology is now being tested, which may aid social welfare services staff using, say, palmtop or laptop computers to link with their networks by high-speed radio networks. No wires are needed and Wi-Fi operates via public 'hot-spot' locations where people can gain broadband Internet access. Initially, with the main usage seen to be in the private sector, these points of access are being located in hotels and airports (Parkinson, 2003c). Yet, in pilot Wi-Fi areas such as the Westminster project in London, once radio transmitters are installed in a number of roads there will be identifiable locations at which public services staff can maintain contact, access data and send data back to their office (ICT system) on a mobile, palm-held tablet or laptop (Ryle, 2003, p 6). Initially, this is envisaged to be most useful for traffic wardens and environment inspectors, but the principle could be extended to social workers, probation officer or community outreach workers (Digital Home, 2003, p 26).

From back-office to front-office: geographic information systems

Geographic information systems (GIS) have been defined, at their basic level, as "a computerized system for storing, retrieving, analyzing, and displaying geographic data" (Monmonier, 2002, p 3). From the 1990s, this spatial tool, combined with ICT management of data, began to offer planning and highways departments a new dimension to information management. GIS designed for crime analysis was then developed to help identify high-crime areas. The key extra benefit was that combining textual data in a graphical format allowed it to be displayed and visualised – and hence conceptualised and understood – more effectively than is possible with tabular methods of presenting information. GIS cuts across (vertical) application systems – such as various databases of socioeconomic indicators of need – in order to provide a clearer picture (or 'patterning') (see Figure 3.2).

Within a single organisation, such as a local authority, data are held on operational systems relating to council tax, electoral registration, housing benefit and social services. By the mid-1990s, social welfare agencies had begun to use GIS software, with the support of planners' technical expertise, in pilot projects to integrate data on various aspects of 'need': for example, data from a range of administrative data sets and data on resource allocation (from other social service client databases) could be 'spatially referenced' to aid planning and delivery of services (Noble and Smith, 1994, pp 360, 374).

Robertson and Wier (1998, pp 224-34) described an innovative project in Missouri, which illustrated how GIS maps could "enable practitioners to integrate neighbourhood information into their direct service provision". Key advantages were that:

- maps can make it possible to quickly identify trends within a data set;
- interactive maps can allow the user to make queries and explore, visually, emerging patterns; and
- the information management function helps the caseworker identify which resources are appropriate and available in the neighbourhood for a given client.

For various social welfare fields, the UK 2001 Census (released in 2002) offers the potential to apply GIS to Census data and Office for National Statistics neighbourhood statistics to provide a much 'richer' picture of socioeconomic indicators at the local authority and ward levels (Hughes et al, 2002, p 61). This will assist health promotion, social security and local education authority planners, among others, to target areas and refine approaches to tackle social exclusion.

Finally, innovative examples of using (back-office) GIS to support (front-office) public services applications are now evident. Boxes 5.9 and 5.10 illustrate two such examples in the UK.

Back-office integration with the front office: the NHS example

Building back-office integration within the NHS

Initial IT projects in the NHS in the 1980s and early 1990s focused on 'basic issues such as the inadequacy of local data collection mechanisms' (Politt et al, 1991); later initiatives – the Information Management and Technology Strategy, 1992 – added the 'C' of communication into ICT and began the shift towards intranet and extranet development across the health service. During the 1990s, this began with linking all health authorities, NHS trusts, the NHS Executive and Department of Health by e-mail, and then evolved to establish NHS*net*.

Box 5.9: Customer relationship management and geographic information systems (GIS) at Tower Hamlets

GIS is included as an integral element of a new customer relationship management (CRM) system within the London borough of Tower Hamlets' e-government strategy. In early 2002, a CRM system was implemented to enable call centre operators to log service requests and provide information to callers. The initial focus was on street services and parking. In the second phase, CRM will include services relating to environmental health and trading standards and corporate complaints. GIS has been applied across a number of departments, including education, neighbourhood regeneration and planning. It supports what have been identified as the key borough databases: the land and property gazetteer, a people database and an organisational database. Accordingly, call-centre staff can deal with enquiries with the visual aid of seeing, in a web-based format, the citizen's location, which will link with the ability to make or request the appropriate response in spatial and service terms.

Source: ESRI (2003)

Box 5.10: MAGUS

MAGUS is an innovative project that has developed, tested and applied a GIS-based system for modelling access for wheelchair users in urban environments. In essence, it provides both urban planners and disabled people with up-to-date, detailed and customised information to help them plan and manage their access and mobility in the public realm. For the planners, MAGUS has the capability to provide information that will assist with road building and provision for dropped kerbs, for example, to improve disabled people's access. In turn, wheelchair users can be offered a fully interactive, route-finding device to enable individuals 'to assess, compare and select routes through urban areas, based upon their own circumstances and need'. Currently, the programme is on a CD ROM that can be run through a PC; the aim is that it will be web-based, so that it can be used via hand-held devices that link via the Internet to a central server.

Source: Matthews et al (2003, pp 34, 44)

This system enabled effective sharing of information between the NHS and other health organisations to create, in effect, a very large intranet. Accordingly, by February 2001, 88% of general practices had an NHS*net* line installed, which linked to 100% of health authorities and 97% of hospital and community health trusts (NHS, 2001).

ICT in the NHS is explored further below by examining current and planned developments of telemedicine; computer mediation communication; the development of NHS Direct Online; and the vision of future developments.

Telemedicine

'Telemedicine' (or 'telecare') refers to a number of ways in which patients and clinicians can be 'connected' through ICT, including by video conferencing, digitised stored images and the Internet. The aim is that some healthcare can be provided remotely by telemedicine, with benefits of improved quality of care, reduction in health inequalities (relating, say, to geography) and cost effectiveness (Mair, 2001, p 13).

From 2000, UK health authorities began to test the feasibility of telemedicine systems. One pilot began in a north Manchester primary care group in 1999, described in Box 5.11, while an international example linking health and social services is set out in Box 5.12.

In parallel, various 'telehealth' approaches are being piloted in the UK, whereby patients with certain conditions (such as sleep apnoea) can stay at home with

Box 5.11: UK telemedicine example

Nurses working for a specialist contractor visit GPs' surgeries, photograph patients' skin ailments with a digital camera and store electronic images on their laptops. Data is then downloaded to specialist dermatologists who can decide which patients need further treatment. Such 'teleconsultations' have resulted in cost savings for the NHS and have reduced the average waiting time for a dermatology appointment from 18 months to 17 days.

Source: Cross (2000, p 2)

Box 5.12: US telemedicine example

Through an interactive video teleconferencing system, doctors and nurse practitioners in one part of the state of Florida can undertake an abuse evaluation of a child with the child protection team based elsewhere. A nurse, standing with the patient, serves as the examiner's hands, moving a hand-held camera over the patient's body. A special camera allows the doctor to see the patient, and vice versa, in 'real time' on monitors. This system lessens the child's trauma by making long trips unnecessary, while the agencies can build stronger cases against offenders when examinations are completed quickly by specially trained professionals.

Source: Ross (2001)

the essential information being monitored with the use of portable equipment and automatically transmitted to the hospital consultant. Substantial time and cost savings are made by the NHS, while the patients' lives are less disrupted and, in particular, those in remote, rural locations do not lose out on the support networks of family and friends when hospitalised in a distant city (Timms, 2003, p 12).

Computer-mediated communication in health

The National Service Framework in the NHS guides implementation of computer-mediated communication (CMC). A key principle of CMC is that health workers utilise electronic systems only if they are seen as offering "a clear solution to a clinical or professional issue rather than being technologically driven" (Brooks et al, 2001, pp 63-4). A response to the mobile and time-constrained patterns of health professionals' lives, CMC is built on 'asynchronous electronic communication' tools – such as e-mail and text-based conference systems – enabling users to engage and interact with colleagues at convenient times. A recent study of CMC has shown a shift in usage from mainly e-mail 'flyers' on study days or the scheduling of meetings to more discursive e-mails related to clinical knowledge and practice (Brooks et al, 2001, p 65).

Evolution of NHS Direct

As is the case in the US, it is likely that e-mail will increasingly be used for communication between patients and physicians. Hughes et al note that, as information becomes known about a certain condition, it could be circulated directly to patients who are assessed to be at high risk of developing it. Similarly, at times of intense interest in a particular topic – which could be measured via NHS Direct statistics of numbers of 'hits' – targeted information could be sent to registered patients (Hughes et al, 2002, p 55).

A personal 'healthspace' for users of NHS Direct Online (www.nhsdirect.nhs.uk) is being developed during 2003 as a secure, customisable area of the health advice website where people can store private, personal information and advice (such as blood group, medication, allergies and medical appointments). It could also act as an electronic 'mailbox' for health news of interest to the user and for confidential e-mail responses from health professionals to requests submitted to the site's online enquiry service. Users would have the option to share access with a health professional, relative or carer if they wished (*Future Health Bulletin*, 2003a). The head of the *NHSnet* project has indicated that the next priority is to meet "the pressing need in some sections of the NHS for mobile access to the *NHSnet* service" (see Chapter Four) (Gold, 2003, p 23).

Future developments: one NHS system, one patient record

With the National Strategic Programme for IT in the NHS (2002), the plan is to move away from multiple information systems based primarily on organisational structures 'to a situation in which professionals are provided access to the one integrated system' in the health service. At the centre of this vision is the National Electronic Booking System (see Box 5.13).

Over organisations: portals

Internet 'portals' are increasingly becoming the tool whereby government presents its online information. In essence, a portal is a single point of access, where services are listed in one place that is easy to access and easy to use (Pleace and Quilgars, 2002, p 2). In particular, government portals seek to present this single gateway "based around life episodes or other customer oriented subjects" (LondonConnects, 2001, p 36) rather than by functional silos of government departments. In common with commercial portals, a key ingredient is that they seek the role of "trusted guide" to steer people to other websites, based on their having a strong brand and a lot of information about their customers (Cairncross, 2001, p 116).

However, progress is slow on the main UK government portal, UK Online. Most of the five million hits a week (in 2002) are seeking information rather than being transactional. This is illustrated by the way that individual government departments remain in their 'silos' so that an individual setting up a business or reporting a death in the family still cannot fill out one electronic form rather

---

Box 5.13: NHS National Electronic Booking System and Integrated Care Records Service

In essence, the National Electronic Booking System would enable GPs routinely to book patients needing minor surgery directly into hospital. This would also allow the patient to choose a hospital as well as a convenient time. The software to be introduced into GPs' surgeries will connect them to acute, community and mental health hospitals. Information will also flow in the other direction, with 'electronic data exchange' dispatching, for example, pathology and radiology results from hospitals automatically to GPs' computer screens. The first electronic bookings of hospital appointments are expected in summer 2004, with roll-out across England by the end of 2005. A parallel development project is the Integrated Care Records Service. This is a scheme, with a longer development timescale, whereby every citizen would have a lifelong medical record available 24 hours a day online for use by GPs, accident and emergency staff and paramedics.

Sources: DoH (2002, 2003); Browne (2000); NHS (2001); Ross (2001)

---

than several paper ones for each department concerned (Sarson, 2002, p 170). As a result, UK Online will close in early 2004 marking the demise of the 'life episodes' model as a way to guide citizens to the right part of government. The planned, replacement – Online Government Store – will group services together in six new categories, including 'health and well being' and 'home and community' (*E-Government Bulletin*, 2003b).

Box 5.14 shows, though, that the prize is worth seeking by considering the development of the Canadian government website.

Box 5.14: The Canadian government website

Canada ranks top in the Accenture study of government websites' 'maturity'. The site is based around 'audience gateways', and the numerous transactional services available include online tax payment by citizens and postal account management by businesses. In its development phase, the goals were redefined, 'from putting all services online to only those that are most commonly used'. In its fifth year, in 2003, ongoing review is led by a regular citizens' panel that collects data on user preferences, as well as quarterly focus groups. Ultimately, the best success criterion is usage, and approximately 50% of all Canadians have visited the website (compared with the equivalent UK figure of around 10%).

Sources: Hill (2003, p 11); www.canada.gc.ca

'Sub-portals' for more specialised areas are also being developed. Run by the Department for Education and Skills, *ChildcareLink* (www.childcarelink.gov.uk) is a national childcare directory and early years information service. As well as being part of UK Online, it is accessible via (BskyB's) digital satellite platform and the local classified directory, *UpMyStreet* (www.upmystreet.com).

By serving particular geographical or regional areas and/or specific communities of interest – such as young people, black and minority ethnic (BME) groups and women – the portal concept has been embraced in the voluntary sector, often with government and private sector support. Two examples are provided in Boxes 5.15 and 5.16.

The key criteria of success in ICT integration in social welfare services are how well a citizen is matched with the specific services relevant to his or her needs, and by improvements in the way that service information relevant to a group of citizens or on issues is made accessible 'in one place'.

Direct, front-office transactions in public and social welfare services are still in development and are currently most advanced for online payment of council tax, registering for schools or accessing lists of childcare providers. This chapter has noted the potential role of back-office IT systems supporting service delivery at the front-office interface with users of even the most complex and sensitive

Box 5.15: Youngscot.org

Youngscot.org is a National Youth Information Portal for Scotland, containing over 2,000 pages of information for 12- to 25-year-olds covering education, work, training, housing, health, travel, volunteering and leisure. It is funded by the Scottish Executive, matched by business and national agencies. The 'Ur 'Say Channel' offers a chat-room facility, which is developed with the Scottish Youth Parliament and International Teledemocracy Centre. Young people provide content on news and events in their local area, which can be streamed to registered site users who have created a portal personalised to their community and interests. Developments include an SMS text alert service and designing a version of the site for interactive digital television. There are links with a printed newspaper version, *youngscot*; a free, confidential legal advice line; and a Post Office Young Scot Action Fund (for small grants). Strong web safety guidelines are built in, including to address 'text bullying'.

Sources: Young Scot Enterprise (nd); www.youngscot.org

Box 5.16: HEROS

HEROS is a regional information portal – Hull and East Riding Options – managed by the North Bank Forum for Voluntary Organisations. The site, launched in 2001, acts as a gateway to health, social care and legal information for all ages. Straightforward 'life event' categories signpost users to the main information on Home, Help, Crisis, Living, Health and Youth across 400 content pages. There are over 500 links to other local and national sites. With Health Action Zone and Community Legal Advice Services funding, there is a focus on information for mental health service users and civil law guidance. The site has a home page link to www.refugeeaccess.info, a website for asylum seekers, refugees and agencies working in Yorkshire and Humberside.

Source: www.heros.org.uk

areas of social welfare. Nevertheless, "it will be much more difficult to replicate through a portal the steps needed to provide care-based services" in elderly care, housing accommodation and child protection (Deloitte Research, 2001, p 15).

In this chapter, the significance of the 'value chain' in information management has been outlined, which provided the context for exploring three core aspects of information integration: *within* the organisation, *between* organisations, and *over* organisations.

In Chapter Six, theories of organisational and service development will be examined, while central aspects of the 'digital divide' and e-government will be taken up in Chapters Seven and Eight respectively.

Thinklist

- **What is your information chain? Where are the breaks and duplications?**
- **What is the information chain between your front office and back office; between your workplace and partner agencies; over your agency and your partner agencies?**
- **How could this be improved?**

SIX

People, organisations and ICT

Introduction

This chapter sets out to demonstrate:

- the development of an ICT strategy from the basis of an information management strategy and the differences between the two;
- the importance of recognising that ICT development is rooted in a social context;
- that ICT is increasingly necessary but rarely sufficient for meeting organisational objectives;
- that an ICT strategy should not necessarily be equated with additional expenditure on ICT; and
- the stages and techniques of ICT systems' design and delivery, investment and costing, appraisal and review.

The chapter summarises the issues for ongoing management of the organisation's ICT systems. Finally, some themes are drawn together that collectively highlight some of the key ingredients of failure. But a salutary way to start considering these issues is with some statistics about ICT investment.

ICT investment: a panacea for success?

In March 2003, the trade magazine *Computing* reported on a leaked UK government report on IT. The *Guardian* reported the story thus: 'Government faces £1.5 billion bill for IT failures' (http://politics.guardian.co.uk). Failed projects included:

- Pathway: smartcards for benefits payments in 1998/99. Cost: £698 million. Project cancelled.
- Prison Service 1999. The Home Office drew up plans to overhaul prisons' IT and then scrapped them – at a cost of £8 million.
- Immigration and Nationality Directorate 2001. The IT project was cancelled because the system was over-complex. Cost: £77 million.
- Probation Service 2001. Work on the system was suspended after costs came in 70% above budget. Estimated waste: £118 million.
- Child Support Agency 2001/02. £50 million overspend due to changes in system.

- Individual Learning Accounts 2001/02. Flagship training scheme – project cancelled amid accusations of fraud. Estimated waste: £66.9 million.
- Libra. Plan to link magistrates courts renegotiated, but only after £134 million wasted.

The report was hotly contested by government spokespeople:

> *Computing* magazine's claims to have a leaked document are misleading, inaccurate and mischievous ... IT projects failed long before this government came into office. The Government is now taking a number of steps to deal with this. (Sky News, 2003)

Quite apart from the documented failures, ICT expenditure may not produce any positive effects. The Audit Commission put it like this: "... computers which should have improved public services, may seem only to have changed them" (Audit Commission, 1994, p 3).

ICT failure is too often associated with large public sector organisations. In fact, ICT failures are associated with organisations of all sizes (see Ticher et al, 2002). Similarly, the casual newspaper reader may conclude that failures in ICT are the exclusive preserve of the public sector. The reality is rather different: the private sector makes similar mistakes to those in the public and voluntary sectors (see, for example, Heeks, 1999, p 58). According to *The Economist* (1998, p 21), "Robert Solow, a Nobel-prize-winning economist, once remarked that: 'you can see computers everywhere but in the productivity statistics'". The apparent absence of a productivity boost from the new technology has come to be known among economists as the 'productivity paradox' (*The Economist* article offers several reasons for the apparent paradox; see also Cairncross, 2001).

Such failures are not due to random forces. Patterns have been identified in the actions that increase or reduce the chances of ICT failure. Some starting points to try to avoid ICT problems – or at least reduce the scale of the failures – are outlined below.

Information management strategy versus ICT strategy

Chapter Four set out the elements of an IMS and the fundamental questions to be addressed as part of this process. A key consideration in the information management strategy was what was called the three 'S's: service users, staff, stakeholders.

It is important to emphasise again that an ICT strategy is subsidiary to an information management strategy because it derives from it. An effective ICT strategy cannot be developed in isolation from the IMS.

As was emphasised earlier, it may be a conscious, formal and entirely valid decision not to use ICT systems in the management of information generally or of certain specific areas of information. Indeed, it is worth having an IMS even if there are no plans to develop an ICT strategy. ICT systems must be cheaper, more efficient or add value (see Chapter Five) to existing information management systems.

In Chapter One, it was observed that public responses to new technologies (the steam engine, telephone, television) could help us understand responses to ICT. Indeed, the four responses can be caricatured as: hoping it goes away, total cynicism, total belief, and as a useful part of a wider whole. These perspectives are reflected in the workplace. In describing the role of ICT (or simply 'IT', as he calls it) in organisational and service improvement (what he calls 'reform'), Heeks identifies four 'I's:

- Ignore. Public officials are ignorant about IT and information systems. They therefore do not include consideration of either in their plans for reform....
- Isolate ... investment in IT is therefore included in reform plans but is seen as the responsibility of IT experts ... for other reform agendas, it is added as an afterthought ... and is not linked in any systemic way to the process of reform....
- Idolise ... the public sector becomes awash with IT-driven reform projects which place technology at the heart of the change process....
- Integrate ... it is seen as valuable means to achieve certain reforms but not as an end in itself.... (Heeks, 1999, p 26)

MacKenzie (1999) introduces an interesting twist to this with his model of the 'certainty trough'. This is essentially a research model that demonstrates the old adage that a little knowledge is a dangerous thing. The research shows that scepticism about the benefits of ICT is highest among those who know least about ICT *and* those who know most about ICT. People who know a little about ICT are most optimistic and enthusiastic about the benefits it brings. MacKenzie attributes the high level of scepticism about ICT among those who know most about it to their experience of its limitations. The term 'trough' refers to the low point of the scepticism curve on the graph – the point associated with ICT 'believers' – located between the two high points. This graph may tell us something about the enthusiasm with which politicians have embraced e-government (see Chapter Eight), and the dynamic this promises will be dealt with in Chapter Nine.

Chapter One showed how different workplace cultures can produce different attitudes to ICT, and it seems reasonable to assume that some professional cultures have adopted ICT faster than others. Within this different individuals will be at different points in the certainty trough; as Heeks (1999, p 28) puts it, "ignore can be found next to integrate in the same office corridor".

In Chapter One the idea was introduced that different socioeconomic groups, and men and women have different exposure and attitudes to ICT equipment, skills and training. These statistics and the consequences are explored in more detail in Chapter Seven. The reality is, then, that some of these differences will be reflected in the workplace: a workplace dominated by white AB males will react differently (say) to a workplace in which women – with a range of minority ethnic backgrounds – make up the larger share of the workforce.

The evolving ICT strategy will arise from, and have to take account of, the different workplace cultures. It makes sense to take this into account as the ICT strategy process described below unfolds.

Organisational effectiveness

Different cultural views about the efficacy of ICT can spill over into judgements about the efficacy of the organisation. Such views can range from espousing the imperative to embrace ICT as the key to better services (see Chapter Eight) to arguing that ICT is an attempt to reinforce what is wrong in social welfare (Henman and Adler, 2003; Huntingdon and Sapey, 2003). The reality often lies between these two extremes.

Tameside (www.tameside.gov.uk) claims to be the first local authority to meet the e-services government target (that is, all services are available online), some two years ahead of schedule. As reporter Michael Cross wrote:

> Now one council has cracked the 2005 e-government target, can the UK's other 467 local authorities get there simply by cloning its website? Sadly not. Tameside.gov.uk is no Potemkin facade over a decaying municipal structure but an *integral* part of 10 years modernisation. (Cross, 2003a; emphasis added)

Indeed, in those organisations that have had clear success in meeting organisational objectives, while ICT is clearly identified as a factor it is ranked so low as to not actually appear in the analysis (see Box 6.1).

However, ICT in service delivery cannot be ignored. London Advice Services Alliance (lasa), writing in relation to the voluntary sector, put it like this:

> The starting point for this study was that voluntary organisations ignore information and communication technologies (ICT) at their peril ... [b]ut increasingly, the two strands of ICT – 'doing things better' and 'doing better things' – make the difference between an organisation that is able to achieve its aims ... and one that is seen to be falling behind. (Ticher et al, 2002)

In a helpful summary, Henman and Adler link the historic development of welfare over the past 150 years with the development of new technologies:

> Mechanical information technologies such as adding machines, ledger machines, typewriters and sorting and enveloping machines were progressively introduced from the 1920s to the 1950s to more or less mechanize activities undertaken by humans. (Henman and Adler, 2003, p 147)

If nothing else, the sheer scale of welfare undertakings demands mechanisation – currently provided through ICT. The figures given in Figure 1.1 about NHS Direct give some idea of this; but perhaps the last word among information handlers should be given to the tax service. According to Terry Hawes, head of e-service development at the Inland Revenue, the service has the biggest customer base of any UK organisation, receiving every year nine million tax returns, 45 million end-of-year employee tax returns, and over 100 million letters, forms and telephone calls (Hawes, 2003).

One way of summarising this is to say that ICT is necessary in an organisation – but not sufficient. And adopting the correct form of ICT is best done through an ICT strategy.

Box 6.1: Housing Benefit administration

According to an article in *Housing Today* (21 November, 2002), the London borough of Camden took five days to process a benefit claim; this was in contrast to Tower Hamlets (6.59 days), Haringey (14.05 days), Wandsworth (17.16 days), Brent (22.36 days), Hammersmith and Fulham (22.9 days), Islington (24 days), Greenwich (27.8 days), Lewisham (28 days), Southwark (32 days), Hackney (49 days), Westminster (71 days). (Figures have been drawn from the Audit Commission's best value performance indicators 2000/01.) Awaiting the outcome of a rent decision can be a stressful business – after all, an individual's housing depends on it – so the difference between a five-day wait and a 71-day wait is significant. Further, the article showed that there was a significant difference between the cost of administration per claim, ranging from the cheapest (Camden at £72.41 per claim) to the most expensive (Islington at £161.78 per claim). While the report acknowledges the problems around outsourcing work to some private contractors, other local authorities – like Camden itself – have their processes firmly in-house. Interestingly, the article argues: "The secret to Camden's success lies in team organisation, having staff who know the job and are committed to the work, and close working relationships with other parties such as housing associations and advice bureaux". Throughout the article, ICT is not mentioned once (Chatterjee, 2002).

Elements of an ICT strategy

There are four elements in developing an ICT strategy:

- the element of planning and prioritisation;
- the social element: the three 'P's of people, processes, policies;
- the financial element: issues around efficiency, effectiveness and added value; and
- the design and delivery element: the process of project management.

Each element is considered in turn (for detailed perspectives on ICT strategy formulation see, for example, Earl, 1989; Daniels, 1994; Edwards et al, 1995).

Planning and prioritisation

In Chapter Four, Earl's model 'IS strategy formulation: a multiple methodology' (Earl, 1989, p 71) was introduced. His contention is that there should be three main thrusts:

* top-down ('Where we'd like to be');
* bottom-up ('Where we are'); and
* inside out ('Creative responses').

In Chapter Four, this approach was applied to the information management strategy. It can equally well be applied to the ICT strategy. For example, top-down might start looking at how new capabilities of ICT help the organisation (department, team) achieve its goals.

Bottom-up takes into account where the organisation is in terms of its existing ICT provision and what might be the next logical step (and the step after that). While in an ideal world the top-down approach might favour a completely different ICT system, the realities of previous expenditure may mean that the existing system is a given: so-called sunk costs. The bottom-up approach is essentially incremental. Indeed, a link can be made here to Nolan's typography (1987) that was introduced in Chapter Three: "The management challenge therefore is to anticipate the next stage and avoid either an excessive crisis or undue retardation in the evolution" (Earl, 1989, p 29).

Inside out can apply either to an organisation-wide perspective (for example, the one-stop shop in the 'Prevention through Communication' case study in Chapter Three) or to individuals. Earl calls these individuals "brightsparks and product champions" (Earl, 1989, p 29). Another term might be 'techies' or 'super users'. These individuals are those who do not have ICT in their formal job description (or at least no more than anyone else) but who nonetheless take it upon themselves to improve their own knowledge and to aid other staff – and by extension the wider organisation – with ICT matters. A higher-order techie or super user is one who is conversant enough with both ICT and the team/organisation objectives to come up with genuinely creative responses to IMS and the ICT strategy. Furthermore, very few organisations can afford to squander their existing resources: it makes sense, then, to harness those super users and techies to the inside-out element of the ICT strategy.

In Chapter Four, the issue of prioritisation and risk was introduced. Not everything can be achieved at once. How should the different risks be weighted and prioritised (Daniels, 1994, pp 107-8)? If the organisation is new and the success of the organisation is predicated on ICT systems that go live on a certain day – for example, through primary legislation (such as the Criminal Records Bureau, the Child Support Agency) – then there may be little choice but to go for the 'big bang' approach: a universal system for the entire organisation. However, big bangs can result in big crashes, crippling the organisation. It may be preferable – unless it is unavoidable – to go for the slow, steady and incremental approach in order to minimise risk. So-called scalability, in which the different blocks of the ICT system can be assembled piece by piece, is an important concept.

The social element: the three 'P's

ICT systems are embedded in social systems. Thus, the second element in the ICT strategy is what can be called the three 'P's: people, processes, policies. A significant shift in ICT capability might have a significant impact on people, the way they work, the tasks before them and the policies they adhere to. People may simply feel anxious; one of the authors remembers his request for a PC being opposed by the head of administration in the department on the grounds that it would reduce work for the typing pool and eventually put them out of a job (this was in 1992). Or it might prompt a significant change of role at work (see Box 6.2).

All of the housing associations featured in Box 6.2 successfully managed to change the roles of affected staff without adverse effects. Nevertheless, the difficulty of making a shift in work patterns should not be underestimated. Similarly, the introduction of new ICT systems should trigger reviews of existing processes and policies. Without such reviews, existing processes and policies can be effectively 'beached' leaving staff in difficult situations (see, for example, Regan, 2003). The mutual interaction of significant ICT changes on the three 'P's and of the three 'P's on ICT should not be underestimated.

On a larger scale, the introduction of ICT changes can have a profound impact on large numbers of people and many national organisations. A good recent example is the changes taking place in banking and the way people receive their benefits. Reynolds has pointed out that in 1999 the government planned to 'move all benefits payments from giro to automated credit payments (ACT) by 2003 thus saving the government approximately £650 million a year in administration costs and fraud'. Payments have to be made into an account, but "some 6-9% of individuals do not have any bank or building society account and 14-23% live without the flexibility of a current account" (Reynolds, 2003, p 12).

The precise correlation between those wholly dependent on benefits and those without a bank account is unknown; but it is likely to be high. The Post Office is introducing a 'no frills' account (POCA) and some 18 financial institutions have also developed basic accounts. A phased process is under way to move several hundred thousand people (starting from 1 April 2003) into basic bank accounts for often the first time in their lives.

Box 6.2: From face-to-face contact to telephone call centre?

Call centres are more than simply a fancy name for a bunch of phones in one room (for example, Dutton, 2001, p 153). They can offer reduced rates to callers, 24-hour service seven days a week, provide call handlers with instant database details on the caller, prioritise calls, and offer sophisticated screening and handling systems, and automatic transfer to other geographically distant centres.

Housing Today explored the trend among housing associations to scale down traditional over-the-counter transactions in estates offices and to move to dealing with housing problems by telephone and rent collection via swipe cards at post offices, phone or Girobank website. Katie Puckett (2003, p 26) writes:

> Last month, the William Sutton Trust said it was considering closing
> 25 of its 60 estate offices as the result of a new card payment
> scheme for rent collection. Over-the-counter payments occupy a fifth
> of staff time at the Trust's offices but this manual chore will be
> phased out by July.... East Thames shut its six area offices and moved
> staff into its headquarters.... 'There was an amount of trepidation
> [said a spokesperson for East Thames] ... it was a fairly big change and
> we were creating roles that many housing associations don't have.
> People weren't sure, especially if they'd been working in traditional
> associations for a long time ...'. The Housing Association Circle 33
> now takes 200,000 calls a year and receives 96% of customer contact
> by the telephone, with paper and electronic communications
> commanding only 2% each.

Efficiency, effectiveness, adding value

The third element in developing an ICT strategy concerns issues of efficiency, effectiveness and adding value; concepts that were introduced in Chapter Five. The ICT strategy should address the question: which types of gathering, managing, storing, retrieving and transmitting information can be supported by ICT in ways that are cheaper and more efficient, and that add value to existing processes?

Before unpacking this task, though, some possible assumptions need to be dispelled. It is commonly believed that an ICT strategy equates with (a) computers per se, (b) expenditure on computers through both the upgrading of existing hardware and software, and (c) acquiring new computers. This is not necessarily the case (see Box 6.3).

The ICT strategy in Box 6.3 is contrary to some common expectations of what an ICT strategy might comprise. Overall, the strategy planned to save money on existing ICT rather than spend more on ICT by offsetting expenditure

---

Box 6.3: An ICT strategy for a medium-sized voluntary organisation

A voluntary sector organisation convened an ICT strategy group for the first time. ICT use and skills varied considerably throughout the organisation, from individuals with non-existent skills and no experience to those using small networks effectively. After the initial meetings the group identified three priorities:

- The 'call-carrier' (that is, the firm that supplied voice and Internet provision) was to be transferred from BT to another telecom company. This was expected to save 20% per year on telephone charges and came with a free internal digital exchange that allowed additional facilities that the organisation did not previously possess. Criteria met: cheaper, more efficient and added value (for example, direct dial).
- Staff and their ICT provision were distributed over a number of buildings on a small site. File sharing would improve organisational effectiveness. Further, costs through multiple individual ISP accounts were high as well as being inefficient. However, wiring up a network between buildings would have been prohibitively expensive. The other solution was an intranet, which would have been accessed remotely. This would have been expensive to establish and would require significant development of staff skill sets to use effectively, while installing multiple broadband sockets would be expensive and inflexible. The possibility of a wireless network was also explored but rejected on the grounds that it was still an emerging technology and the organisation did not want the risk of piloting one of the new 'Wi-Fi' systems (for example, Firewire, Bluetooth) over another. Instead, one new office building was becoming available. All staff who were ICT-dependent would move to this one office. (This met other organisational goals too.) This one office would be cabled, allowing a network. All the existing outside lines to individuals' ISP accounts would be cancelled and replaced by one ADSL connection in the new office. This was expected to save a small amount of money in the first year; in addition, download time would decrease and staff would be saved the time and inconvenience of regular dial-up during working hours. Criteria met: cheaper and more efficient.
- A handful of the staff had PCs that were too old to 'participate' in the network. These machines would be replaced – however, minimum specification for participation in a network was moderate, so all other PCs were judged to be adequate if not 'high-end'.

against savings. Of the reallocated expenditure, it was planned to spend only a small proportion on computers. Upgrades of software are avoided unless essential.

A helpful tool is the cost–benefit analysis. How great are the benefits? Do they really justify the cost? One of the authors has a personal organiser – on paper. Back-up is provided by software on the home PC. Thus, address lists are updated and printed off as necessary. He could invest in a personal digital assistant but calculates that the financial outlay plus the time involved in learning a new system (the costs) greatly exceeds any advantages he might derive from the new system (the benefits).

Design and delivery

The fourth element is around design and delivery – project management. Project management is an effective mechanism for specifying and then installing an ICT system (see, for example, Slack et al, 1995, ch 16). The term 'project management' is often used loosely, but in fact the concept has tightly defined characteristics: "A project is a set of activities which have a defined start point and a defined end state, pursue a defined goal and use a defined set of resources" (Slack et al, 1995, p 633).

According to Slack et al, elements of a project include an objective, complexity, uniqueness, uncertainty, and a temporary nature (that is, it has a beginning and eventually an end) (Slack et al, 1995). Projects also have a strong multidisciplinary element. Designing, delivering and developing ICT lend themselves readily to project management techniques (see also www.lasa.org.uk/knowledgebase).

The project needs to be led by a project team. It is too easy for the project team to be made up of individuals who overrepresent one workplace culture at the expense of others. If the team is dominated by 'techies', the project may be of little use to real users; if it is dominated by users, the conceptions of ICT held by the group may be unrealistic. If it is dominated by front-line staff, the system may not connect with the organisation's strategic goals, and, if dominated by strategic staff, the concepts may not be rooted in practical day-to-day reality.

A key role, then, is that of project leader. Project leadership is not about being a 'techie'. It is about people skills: ensuring that the project staff are motivated, resourced and pay attention to the possibilities and constraints. Leaders must facilitate and enable the process while having sufficient authority to make sure the project stays on schedule. Future users should be given the opportunity to sit on the project team. Even if the opportunity is not taken up, it engenders a sense of ownership among affected staff. If bottom-up ownership is important, so is top-down ownership. The most senior levels of the organisation must be committed to the scheme. The Audit Commission put it like this:

> A lack of management commitment often results in project failure. If there is no commitment from the top, then the enthusiasm and motivation of other staff will disintegrate and the project will be at risk. One approach is to appoint a project sponsor in the client department who takes full

responsibility for the success of the project. This must be a senior person....
(Audit Commission, 1994, p 56)

At some point energy and time will need to be put into ensuring the success of the project team (for example, Joyce, 2002). Thus, commitment from the top will translate into real work (Audit Commission, 1994, p 56). One of the authors remembers a director of social services to whom 'commitment' meant erratic, brief but effusive exhortations to elected council members on the benefits of ICT in the department. For the rest of time (particularly when problems occurred in the project process) he was noticeably absent.

Project management can be broken into five stages: establish a need (that is, via the ICT strategy), consider alternatives, commit to one alternative, track progress, and manage outcome (Audit Commission, 1994, p 52). At the second stage, sometimes customised (rather than off-the-shelf) software is considered. While the customised option is tempting for some – and no doubt essential for others – a surprising range of off-the-shelf software is often available. Furthermore, it is cheaper, less likely to have bugs, and can often be used in a trial before purchase (see, for example, 'Small but perfectly informed' 2002). In contrast, with customised software there is a risk that the commissioning team will continually have to add and subtract from the original specification. Where software is being customised in-house, projects develop that are months and years overdue – and are then fit only for the scrap heap; where external consultants are involved, costs can quickly spiral. As the Audit Commission put it: "Past experience has made it clear that the cost of correcting errors found in computer systems grows exponentially as the project progresses" (Audit Commission, 1994, p 56).

These elements of the ICT strategy can now be assembled in schematic form (see Figure 6.1).

Whereas the text and the diagram display a fairly sequential model, the reality is more of an iterative process, with each stage being repeatedly revisited and revised in the light of information and discussion arising from later stages.

Earlier, the point was made that ICT systems are shaped by the social context as well as shaping the social context. In this context, training for the new systems is vital; but the 'training' will have to go well beyond the standardised 'this-is-how-the-new-software-works' approach to examining work policies and practices. If the disparate cultures of the organisation have not 'bought into' whatever new ICT is proposed and the implications, the project is conceivably at risk. Another important element of embedding ownership is explored below.

Cost and expenditure management

A recurring problem, in both top-down and bottom-up approaches, is underestimation of cost. It is a mistake to regard ICT costs as relating only to

Figure 6.1: Developing an ICT strategy

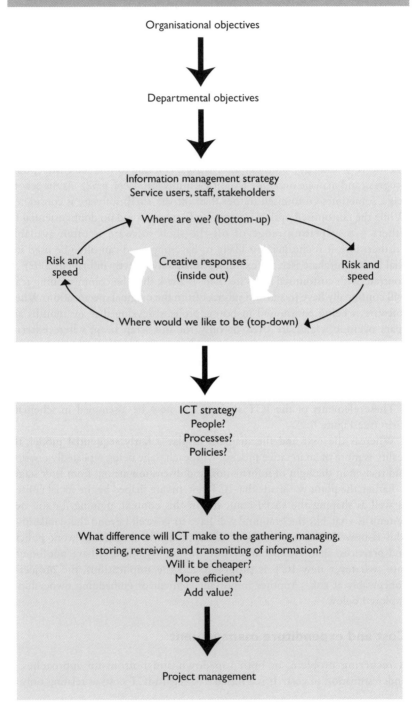

Organisational objectives

Departmental objectives

Information management strategy
Service users, staff, stakeholders

Where are we? (bottom-up)

Risk and
speed

Creative responses
(inside out)

Risk and
speed

Where would we like to be (top-down)

ICT strategy
People?
Processes?
Policies?

What difference will ICT make to the gathering, managing,
storing, retreiving and transmitting of information?
Will it be cheaper?
More efficient?
Add value?

Project management

hardware and software. In reality, costs that are not usually budgeted for might include:

- staffing: management, administration, operations, system support and new developments;
- hardware financing and maintenance costs;
- PC financing, maintenance and software licences;
- networks, including staff support costs and usage charges;
- central establishment charges – physical accommodation and so forth;
- domain registration and server fees (web-hosting costs); and
- consumables, such as printer cartridges and paper (derived from Audit Commission, 1994, p 10).

There is also the cost of meeting the Data Protection legislation (see Chapter Two).

These 'narrow' costs are incurred if the ICT system runs straightforwardly with no further problems and consequent costs. But 'broad' costs might include:

- downtime because of systems failure/computer virus;
- lost or corrupted data;
- stolen machines/loss of password;
- consumables out of stock or no longer available due to hardware 'obsolescence'; and
- illicit use of ICT equipment.

The next point to consider is how the organisation manages the costs of ICT and associated services. This may seem an apparent digression. In fact, since the allocation of cost has a major impact on group and individual behaviour (see, for example, Dyson, 1994; Arnold and Turley, 1996), the method by which organisations pay for ICT is, in fact, a major factor determining the success of ICT in the functioning of the organisations.

In addition, an ICT strategy sits within the realities of the organisation. If the organisation's systems are fundamentally supportive of the strategy, it is likely to succeed; if they are at cross-purposes, the strategy is likely to fail. There are essentially four models of costing and funding ICT:

- as a separate budget heading;
- via an overhead;
- via a devolved budget;
- via a federal solution.

These models are now explored in more detail.

As a separate budget heading

In this model, the ICT department stands apart from the rest of the organisation. It has its own income stream, and expenditure priorities reflect the priorities of the ICT department. This model has two major problems. The first is that there is limited ownership by the rest of the organisation of ICT issues as peddled by the ICT department – so the potential of ICT is not developed. It is then not uncommon for parallel ICT expenditure to develop outside the control of the ICT department.

A possible consequence of this is that the top decision-making group of the organisation soon comes under pressure from other departments arguing that funding for the ICT department should be withdrawn from it and redistributed. One of the authors remembers that in a main council department, although there was a central ICT service (provided by funding from the relevant council committee), the staff in the office concerned had made their own individual and group arrangements because the ICT department was so unresponsive. This meant there were some 17 systems in use – many of them incompatible with each other!

Another issue is the abuse of a free good: where departments do not pay for a service, they tend to use that resource at less than optimum capacity. "[T]he absence of an adequate internal charging mechanism encourages users to ignore the cost implications of altering their IT requirements"(Audit Commission, 1994, p 4).

The overhead

An overhead can be defined as "the total … of costs that cannot be identified with a specific unit" (Dyson, 1994, p 257). Usually, this is taken to mean accommodation costs, gas, telephones, and so on, but, given the difficulties of, say, allocating the costs of a network, ICT costs can be charged for in this way as well. This is essentially a less raw version of the first scenario. The costs of the ICT department are met through charging standardised overheads to other departments. This model has similar problems to the previous one. The overhead is levied regardless of whether the service provided is perceived as good or poor. For the ICT department, the view may take hold that its funding sources are secure and that it will continue to have an income whether it meets the needs of its colleagues or not. Ultimately, the model develops the same problems as the separate budget heading model.

The devolved budget

In this the third model, responsibility for ICT expenditure is formally devolved to all the departments. Theoretically, the advantages are local control, ownership and the ability to consider ICT alongside other costs:

> In the past there have been central budgets for IT developments. This has encouraged departments to regard IT as a 'free good'. If departments are to be responsible for their own IT strategies, they must obtain the financial allocation for themselves. Any investments must be appraised alongside their other, competing requirements for resources – for example, a new housing IT system against actual housing improvements. In this way, departments will be committed to their projects and accountable.... (Audit Commission, 1994, p 50)

However, a situation can quickly develop that is akin to Nolan's typographic category of chaos/contagion (Nolan, 1987). Staff may feel unable to handle ICT issues and budgets, or they may feel their service-specific tasks come first, and ICT issues are awarded insufficient priority. Freed from any co-coordinating constraints, managers and departments acquire a range of incompatible hardware and software ... and then learn the hard way about unidentified costs (see above), inter-departmental failures of ICT standardisation, losses of data, virus attacks, failure to comply with the Data Protection Act and the dangers of not being up to date with software licensing.

The federal solution

This model draws on the experiences of Kent County Council (Audit Commission, 1994, p 47). It attempts to retain the advantages both of centralised ICT (economies of scale, control of standards, integration and critical mass of skills) and of decentralised ICT (user control of priorities, ownership, responsiveness to front-line service needs). Federal ICT is characterised by a functional ICT perspective, a balance between specific service areas, and differing pooled experiences, and aims to capture synergies.

Depending on the size and complexity of the organisation, the precise mechanism for delivering the federal approach will differ. In the small voluntary sector organisation (fewer than 30 staff), the federal model would be delivered by a regular ICT working party agreeing to a collective way forward. In larger organisations (50 to 100), the group might be serviced (but not chaired) by the person with whom the ICT function sits. In still larger organisations, there would be a specific ICT department but services would be provided by a mixture of contracted work from the service departments and ongoing service contracts (for example, help desk) ensuring that the specialist function remained fully integrated and responsive to the mainstream of the organisation.

In larger organisations, the ICT strategy group may then commission one or more project groups to manage the tasks of specifying, identifying and seeing the detailed delivery of the changes in ICT – simply holding a coordination function to itself. In smaller organisations, the ICT strategy group and ICT project group may be the same set of individuals. However, the critical determinant is ensuring the group has a range of skills and perspectives and thus can ensure the ownership of the wider organisation, department or team.

An ongoing process

While a specific project may be a one-off, the process of maintaining ICT systems is not. As Kenyon argues:

> An appropriate analogy might be the purchase and maintenance of a car. Regular maintenance and minor repairs are necessary – and expected – to keep a vehicle operating smoothly. In addition to the petrol needed to run the car (not to mention the yearly expenses of licensing and registration), repairs and tune-ups are needed to avoid a serious breakdown. In the long run, changing the oil every 3,000 miles will cost less than a complete engine overall. (Kenyon, 2002, p 7)

The rule holds true – even the most basic single home-based PC needs a virus checker (updated regularly), the recycle bin emptying, a regular file clear-out to stop the hard disk silting up, the hard disk defragging, and so on. Kenyon goes on to recommend six basic rules (see Box 6.4).

The final step, once the new system is installed, is to review it at regular intervals to assess whether the benefits and costs of the new system identified in the ICT strategy have actually been fulfilled.

Box: 6.4: An ongoing process

Preventive budgeting essentials: 70/30 rule. State-of-the-art technology will only be so for a few months and close to obsolescence in two to three years. Consider total cost of ownership (TCO) when purchasing systems. Only 30% of the total cost of owning a computer system is the initial purchase of hardware software and peripherals. Seventy per cent goes on to technical support, training and upgrades. If a system costs you £1,000, maintaining it will cost £2,500.

Budget for computers every year. A computer needs replacing every three years. Therefore, if you annually allocate money for each workstation (say £700), you will be able to replace computers for a third of the office each year.

Train yourself and your staff. If you invest in your machines, invest in yourselves to make sure you actually get the benefits.

Get a systems administrator. One ratio is one half to one full hour per week per employee for basic systems. Use one consultant. For additional expertise outside your staff's knowledge you need a consultant. One who is familiar with your organisation will do a better job in the long term. Keep a back-up copy of your most valuable data off site. If there is a flood or fire, you can walk into a shop and buy another computer – if you lose your database, no amount of money on earth will bring it back. (Kenyon, 2002, p 7)

When it all goes wrong

ICT is a part of the social medium. Consequently, problems around ICT projects are likely to be located in the social sphere as well as in the technical sphere:

> The causes of failure are rarely technical – most of the factors governing success are the user's responsibility. For example, a survey by KPMG showed that only 7% of failed projects were the result of problems associated with computer hardware or software. (Audit Commission, 1994, p 52)

After this overview, it becomes possible to suggest some of the key ingredients for failure in the field of ICT projects:

- a lack of an information management strategy that is derived from the organisational objectives;
- an ICT strategy that is developed without relation to, or in the absence of, a clear understanding of information management within the organisation;
- a lack of commitment and/or active turf disputes between the different cultures that make up the organisation or its constituent parts. This lack of commitment is reflected in the ICT arena or disputes are actively played out in the decision making and use (or lack of use) around ICT;
- an absence of incentives to adopt new ICT methods and/or the presence of perverse incentives in adopting the new methods;
- a lack of a top-level sponsor or the presence of a sponsor who is committed in word only;
- a project leader who sees the prime focus of the job as technological rather than coordinating, facilitating, building support, seeking consensus;
- an absent, weak or unbalanced project management team; and
- over-engineered customised software.

Thinklist

- **The funding of ICT: what model are you experiencing?**
- **How inclusive is your ICT planning, development and delivery?**
- **Do you have an ICT strategy?**

SEVEN

Information exclusion and the digital divide

Introduction

> We cannot stand aside and have a society divided between information haves and information have-nots, a society with an online superclass and an information underclass. (Gordon Brown, 1999, cited in White, 1999)

This chapter will introduce key themes of the 'digital divide', in terms of information exclusion from access to, and the benefits of, the Internet, relating to income, geography, gender, age, disability and race and ethnicity. The key role of social welfare professionals in guiding and mediating the public's online access to information on, and access to, services – as 'information intermediaries' – will then be outlined.

Defining the digital divide

In its simplest terms, the phrase 'digital divide' is frequently used by policy makers and commentators to refer to the disparity between those who access information and communication technologies (ICT) and those who do not (Foley and Alfonso, 2002; Servon, 2002, p 25).

In 2002, the UK government estimated that 95% of businesses and 98% of schools were online (HM Government, 2002). In 2003, 56% of the population were regular users of the Internet, with 48% of all households having Internet access (Office of the e-Envoy, 2003c). Other studies found that 38% of the adult population had never accessed the Internet (Office of the e-Envoy, 2003a). Within this overall usage, survey data consistently finds major discrepancies in use across social classes.

A broad distinction may be made between socio-personal and socioeconomic factors in determining whether individuals experience a 'digital divide'. The socioeconomic factor can also be conceptualised as *capability*, which embraces both physical *access* channels to the technology (from home, work or the community) and the *skills* to use the technology in order for this access to be realised.

In terms of socio-personal factors, there is a strong rights element (see also Chapter Two). Increasing importance is placed on 'network literacy' in terms of a *right* of access to – and "the capacity to use" – "electronic networks to access resources, to create resources, and to communicate with others" (National Grid for Learning, 1997, p 10). The influential Report of the National Working Party on Social Inclusion in 1997 set out a strong case that, since democratic society requires public information to function, "intrinsic to the Information Society is the notion of certain fundamental rights … [of] access to information and communication channels" (National Working Party on Social Inclusion, 1997, p 7). Information inclusion is "increasingly essential to basic [and effective] citizenship" (*New Statesman*, 2000, p xix), whether in interaction with health and housing services or with bank and other financial services.

In other words, the more an individual has the *access* and *skills*, the greater is the shift towards information inclusion through the narrowing of this digital divide. This, though, cannot solely be analysed at the level of the individual or household according to a single criterion such as income, occupation or education. Crucially, to understand what creates the digital divide and how it can be overcome, it is essential to examine the impact of these socioeconomic and socio-personal factors across different groups in the community. Hence, the subject of analysis must be *digital divides*.

Digital divides

Socioeconomic

> Access to ICT is the new elitism, and a new class of ICT-poor has arisen due to inequalities in both distribution, training and economic stratification. (Chester, 1998, p 21)

A rough rule of thumb calculated by the OECD is that, for every $10,000 increase in household income, the number of homes owning a PC rises by 7% (Cairncross, 2001, p 295). Data from the Office for National Statistics in 2002 show a difference of almost 70 percentage points in Internet take-up between lowest and highest income deciles, a gap that increased from 40 percentage points in 1999. This is almost entirely due to increased take-up in the highest income decile (No 10 Strategy Unit, 2002). Yet, the gap falls to less than 10% when the Internet platform is via digital TV ownership.

In policy terms, this factor has been a key concern in the roll-out of the e-government programme in the UK since the late 1990s (see Chapter Eight). At its outset, the government acknowledged the relationship between equal access and information inclusion, whereby people living in poor neighbourhoods are "much less likely to have access to information and communication technologies" (Social Exclusion Unit, 1998, p 74).

The socioeconomic dimension relates, primarily, to education, skills and employment. The concept of an 'information underclass' is relevant here for employees without the labour market status of 'knowledge workers' (see Chapter One). A self-perpetuating spiral of social exclusion can be identified: if individuals are going to be successful in work, then they need to acquire the

ICT skills to fulfil the growth areas of modern employment (DTI, 2000, p 13). In turn, skills are a key component of ICT access, whether 'soft' skills of information literacy and Internet awareness or 'hard' skills of familiarity with, and confidence in use of, ICT. Those working in occupations like sales, service or production will have much less opportunity for Internet access in their workplace, and likely lower rates of PC ownership and Internet usage at home.

Recent government research found that teleworkers represented 7.4% (2.2 million) of those employed in the UK in 2001, yet the pattern is of "more people working from home for *some of the time*, not more people working only from home" (emphasis added). Three quarters were in the private sector, and predominantly professionals, managers and senior officials or in associate professional and technical occupational groups (Hotopp, 2002, p 1; Bayliss, 2003, p 11). Such professional workers are increasingly equipped not only with home PC-based but also mobile wireless access to the Internet. 'Tablet' PCs – or 3G/2.5G mobile technology – designed to be portable, with wireless connectability, are being developed to allow for the experience of mobile Internet in devices that fit into one's pocket yet 'sync' with one's desktop PC at work or at home. As 'location-independent' workers (Bayliss, 2003, p 11), they will, therefore, have both the *access* and the *skills* to make most use of interactive online channels for work as well as social welfare and leisure purposes.

Nevertheless, community wireless projects are now springing up, at grass-roots level, whereby free or nominal charges are made to individuals to gain broadband Internet access through Wi-Fi networks (see Chapter Five) (Cohen, 2003, pp 14-15). There are also local authority pilot schemes: one of the largest council housing estates in the London borough of Lewisham is to become a 'wireless hot spot'. This will provide all its residents with high-speed Internet connections, e-mail and access to community discussion forums (*E-Government Bulletin*, 2003c).

Finally, the implications of information exclusion are greater still for the unemployed and other people not in the labour market or education. For example, the physical withdrawal of bank and other financial-based services from poorer (inner-city and rural) neighbourhoods has been a trend over the past two decades, as these institutions are shifting access to cheaper (to supply), non-face-to-face customer services via telephone and online banking.

Spatial

The Internet has been "touted as a medium with the capability to collapse distance and to eliminate spatial inequalities" (Servon, 2002, p 9).

Manuel Castells describes the spatial distribution of Internet users on a global level as "the new geography of development". This 'geography' is fragmented according to wealth, technology and power. Within both developed and developing countries, urban areas benefit first from "the diffusion of Internet use … [as] rural areas and small towns considerably lag behind in their access to the new medium". At the global level, the rapid diffusion of the Internet is also uneven – nearly two thirds of Internet users were located in North America and western Europe in September 2000 (Castells, 2001, pp 212, 260).

At the UK level, the least connected districts in December 2001 were Blaenau Gwent and Newport in Wales – both had less than 12% of households connected to the Internet. The three most connected districts were Wokingham, Waverley and mid-Sussex in the South East of England, with more than 55% of households connected to the Internet (Foley and Alfonso, 2002). These 'spatial inequalities' show a correlation with government Indices of Deprivation.

'Broadband' technology allows data to be transferred at high speed, which is particularly useful for downloading large files (music and photographs, for example) and real-time information 'streaming' (for example, live news and sports coverage, other video content and online games). In July 2003, 20% of households reporting, in a National Statistics Omnibus Survey, that they had an Internet connection were using broadband (National Statistics, 2003, p 5). Yet there is unevenness in the roll-out of broadband service provision – due to local telephone exchanges and the increased costs of cable networks in remote areas – which may actually be increasing the digital divide between urban and rural residents. It was estimated by the Office of the e-Envoy that by 2003 15-20% of the UK population would still be excluded from broadband due to their physical location (Hughes et al, 2002, pp 103-6; Sarson, 2002, p 170).

New bodies in each English region are to 'block buy' broadband services for public sector organisations such as schools and the NHS (from October 2003). One of the government's aims is to make it more attractive to telecoms companies to extend their broadband infrastructure to households in rural regions. In this way, in the medium term, greater broadband roll-out may "provide a platform for preserving rural economies and for removing some of the disadvantage of distance which communities in such areas suffer" (DTI, 2003a; Kearns, 2002, p 51).

Gender

One group identified early in the emergence of the Internet revolution as being at risk of information exclusion is "women who are not in education or employment, or whose employment gives them no opportunity to use new IT" (National Working Party on Social Inclusion, 1997, p 23). This may particularly apply to women who are disproportionately to be found in low-skilled, part-time employment. As well as labour market factors, usage is likely to be lower for women in some religious or cultural communities, for whom special arrangements such as home outreach or women-only groups may be needed to enable them to learn ICT skills.

Comparing usage statistics over just four years, though, indicates that this gender discrepancy is falling in significance. The historical gap between usage by men and women has narrowed in the UK, falling from 9 percentage points in 2001 to 3 percentage points in 2002 (No 10 Strategy Unit, 2002). Similarly, in the US, the gap in Internet use between men and women had completely closed by November 2001 (Servon, 2002, p 37).

Age

'Technophobia' does exist for some older people but is by no means universal and is a more complex phenomenon than often realised. Contrary to popular perception, which equates older people with reluctance and fewer opportunities to embrace ICT, the phenomenon of 'silver surfers' is evident. Usage statistics show that many older people can be just as interested in and adaptive to the Internet as younger generations. Government figures from 1999 showed that 11% of regular Internet users were over 50 and that online older people actually spent more time (10 hours) using the Internet than younger people (seven hours) each week (Wintour, 2000, p 10).

At the start of the decade, the Better Government for Older People programme was already highlighting projects across the UK that used ICT via home and public access to improve the lives of older people. These included online directories giving advice on local services and social security benefits, and local Internet networks for friendship (McCartney, 2000, pp 16-17). Accordingly, Age Concern recently reported that 4.6 million people aged 50 and over use computers and four million older people in the UK have Internet access (Hughes et al, 2002, p 84).

Nevertheless, in overall terms, Internet access levels are relatively low in older populations. This is because many older people without home access will have difficulty travelling to public access facilities, while those with deteriorating eyesight or arthritis, for example, may find it physically difficult to use ICT (Hughes et al, 2002, p 83). Potential barriers through disability are discussed later in this section.

At the other end of the spectrum, the opportunities for equal access are now greater for children and young people, both in generational terms and with the current cohort through school ICT provision. In generational terms, access is promoted by children and young people's greater 'network literacy' relative to the rest of the household, defined as "the capacity to use electronic networks to access resources, and to communicate with others" (National Grid for Learning, 1997, p 10). The Internet has become the information medium of first choice for young people because:

- it is less didactic;
- it avoids the potential embarrassment of picking up a leaflet or face-to-face contact with professionals;
- the 'disintermediated' nature of online information culture, in which 'informal communication is more valued', has stronger resonance than more formal media.

(National Working Party on Social Inclusion, 1997, pp 28-9)

Children and young people have greater opportunities at school, especially City Learning Centres specialising in ICT provision, to learn the skills to use ICT. By spring 2003, 99% of UK schools had access to the Internet for staff and pupils (compared with only 28% in 1998) (Hirst, 2003). Indeed, overall, Britain currently has more children online than any other European country – and the under-12s comprise the fastest-growing Internet sector (Nielsen// Net Ratings, 2003).

However, a socioeconomic digital divide may still result where poorer households do not have home access to PCs and the Internet. Research into the lives of disadvantaged young people (aged 13-18) by the Teenage Pregnancy Unit in 2001 found that the majority of those involved in the research did not have Internet access and most were not particularly interested in doing so as it was negatively associated with school or pornography. Yet access to the Internet via mobile phones or digital TV was more readily available to this group, thereby providing clues for future strategies of inclusion (Hughes et al, 2002, pp 86-7).

As for disabled children and young people, online ICT applications can enhance their educational development. Ofsted inspectors have reported on the use of digital photographs and other pictorial material from the Internet as an effective support tool for Key Stage 3 and older pupils with special educational needs. In addition, the Internet and virtual chat rooms can improve the reading skills of pupils with special educational needs (Ofsted, 2001, p 9; DTI, 2000, p 18).

In order to help their children with homework, and increasingly to ensure Internet safety, parents are becoming more familiar with ICT. Guidance is available from a Department for Education and Skills (DfES) website (*Parents Online,* www.parentsonline.gov.uk), designed to help parents understand the educational benefits of the Internet. It contains practical help to download free software and e-mail accounts, as well as giving advice and filtering tools for promoting Internet safety.

Disability

Disabled users are often unnecessarily excluded from websites, as well as other ICT tools, by their design. Mobile phones can be too small for people with certain disabilities and the elderly. A study by the Office of the e-Envoy found that only one quarter of central government websites examined passed a test of compliance with key elements of accessibility guidance (Comptroller and Auditor General, 2003, p 8). Yet, in UK law, the 2002 Disability Discrimination Act effectively adds a legal obligation to the moral obligation of public and private sector bodies to make their websites accessible.

Good practice for users with a visual impairment includes an appropriate font size; simple layout; the option of using a text-only version; the use of descriptive tags to explain the content of pictures; easy-to-use navigation; and little or no use of complex graphics (*E-Government Bulletin,* 2003a). In terms of software tools, from the late 1990s, adaptive technologies became more widely available free or at low cost. For example, 'Browsealoud' is added speech software that can be downloaded free and applied to websites so that users with vision or reading impairments can adjust speed, volume and language according to their needs (*E-Access Bulletin*, 2003).

Poor practice in website design can be remedied and sites made more accessible by following the World Wide Web Consortium's *Accessibility Guidelines*, with standards for private, public and voluntary sectors being laid down in the international Web Accessibility Initiative (www.w3.org/WAI) (Byrne, 2001, p 20). Current web accessibility requirements for UK local authorities and other public service agencies need to be followed (see Kreps, 2003). Free services are available on the *Bobby Online Free Portal*, which allows a web page to be scanned for barriers to accessibility (http://bobby.watchfire.com). In the UK, the Royal National Institute for the Blind offers guidance and its web accessibility audit scheme (*See it Right*) checks sites for ease of use by visually impaired users (www.rnib.org.uk/seeitright) (Poluck, 2003b).

The factors explored in this section do not, of course, operate independently of each other. US data, for example, show that the disparity in Internet access between those with and without disability declines when income levels rise, while increasing with age (Castells, 2001, p 250).

Race and ethnicity

The experience of black and minority ethnic (BME) citizens in accessing public services in the UK has traditionally been one of discrimination, unequal access, inappropriate services and lack of confidence when using corresponding services (Griffin, 1998). Since BME communities are disproportionately resident in deprived neighbourhoods, this exclusion has been compounded by the socioeconomic factors discussed earlier. Unsurprisingly, various studies in the UK have found that minority ethnic groups access and use ICT in considerably lower proportions than white ethnic groups (Greater London Authority et al, 2002, p 18; Global Consulting UK Ltd, 2003).

Just as the public and voluntary sectors translate only a limited range of printed leaflets into the many different UK community languages, the Internet remains a mainly European-language-based medium. Lack of community language facilities at most public access Internet points is a hindrance to those for whom English is not their first language, while other language versions of Internet browsers are not widely available in public access points, such as libraries, kiosks and Internet cafés (Phipps, 2001). More basically, the standard English keyboard is a major hindrance for those whose first written language is not a Latin script. Studies among Hispanic communities in the US show that the predominance of English language websites hinders their desire to use the Internet for practical matters related to employment and social welfare (Castells, 2001, pp 254, 264). In the UK, government research commissioned by the DfES found that most software applications in minority ethnic languages provide a user interface that is a blend of English with the minority ethnic language, thereby requiring the user to have a basic knowledge of English to use the application (Global Consulting UK Ltd, 2003, p 9).

The Society of Information Technology Management annual survey (2002) (www.socitm.gov.uk) of local government websites found that less than 10% of UK council sites currently have provision for any language other than English, such as Asian and Chinese, or Gaelic and Welsh, languages. Accordingly, the Office of the E-envoy recently published guidelines (Office of E-Envoy, 2003c) for UK government websites that cite dual-language links and use of PDF files as best practice. The London Borough of Waltham Forest (www.lbwf.gov.uk), for example, offers information in French, Albanian, Somali, Turkish and Urdu (Fletcher, 2002). NHS Direct Online plans to expand the resources available in languages other than English on the site from early 2004 (*Future Health Bulletin*, 2003b). ICT development support for the voluntary sector may play a role too: the London Advice Services Alliance (lasa) has developed a multilingual website, *Multikulti*, which covers debt, employment, housing, health, immigration issues and welfare benefits, and translates information leaflets into 10 community languages (Ashcroft et al, 2003, pp 6-7).

Information intermediaries

Concept and scope

'Information intermediaries' – who may be various statutory, voluntary and community sector professionals and workers – perform a crucial role in supporting their respective clients in ICT access and usage across all social welfare settings. This does not mean that they are information specialists or ICT experts. The varying role and functions of information intermediaries can best be explained through a series of case studies.

Case study: teachers and pupils

Teachers are key information intermediaries for children and young people using the Internet. As described earlier in the chapter, with virtually all primary and secondary schools in the UK now online, the infrastructure exists for pupils to derive the educational benefits of incorporating ICT in their learning. However, many children and young people do not have the full range of skills and competencies of Internet literacy:

- Many lack basic skills in searching, evaluating and integrating information, through, for example, understanding how hypertext links work (*analytical competence*).
- They do not have awareness of the broader social, cultural, economic and political contexts in which Internet information is produced, which underpins a critical evaluation of the Internet (*contextual knowledge*).

- Their *canonical knowledge* is narrowly delimited, being heavily focused on commercial or global sites and brands.
- Their skills do include *production competence*, yet this is more in relation to peer group communication – such as participating in chat rooms and e-mail – than other kinds of content creation (Livingstone, 2001, pp 9-10).

Since the late 1990s, the UK government has invested resources in training teachers in ICT so that they can better support children "to act upon the information … [on the Internet for] the questioning, navigating and systematising that is required" (Gill, 1996). Subsequently, nearly three quarters (73.4%) of UK teachers surveyed feel confident in their use of ICT (DfES, 2001) and are better equipped to act as information intermediaries for their students. The implication is that teachers may become, in the future, much more like further or higher education tutors acting as co-coordinators, facilitators, guides and mentors (HumanITy, 2003).

Case study: the National Health Service

UK government ICT policy encourages the public to access websites that "provide knowledge about health, illness and best treatment practice". Accordingly, some patients have "become more informed and assertive", seeking to make informed decisions about their health and lifestyle, including attempting to self-diagnose their own ailments (DoH, 1997, p 20; Lenaghan, 1998, p 2). How, though, does the GP manage a situation in which the carer of an Alzheimer's patient comes to the surgery equipped with the latest research finding on an overseas health website (for example, www.healthinsite.gov.au) detailing a new 'wonder drug' that is licensed in that country but is not an approved product in the NHS, or whose prescription in the case of this patient is not sanctioned by the guidelines of the National Institute of Clinical Excellence (NICE)?

Individual citizens and patients with Internet access can find health information 24 hours a day. "There is a clear demand from the public for … electronic access to health and social care services" (Gann, 2000, p 129 and it will become increasingly common for patients to visit their doctor after conducting prior Internet research. This is part of the shift towards "patient empowerment and self-care that is a significant emerging health trend" (Wyatt, 2000, p 112).

Australian research (in 2001) found that 96% of GPs reported having, at some time, been presented with medical information by patients acquired from the Internet (Williams and Maj, 2001, p 82). However, there is no consensus on the primary consequences. Does Internet access giving patients more and better health information lead to "more equal relationships between patients and their doctors" – or is this at the cost of "increased levels of anxiety among patients about the risks and benefits of illness and treatment" (Henwood, 2001, p 5)?

Moreover, material found on websites is often marketing specific pharmaceutical products, which has resulted in a quarter of the UK population that visits such sites requesting brand-name medications from their doctors (Duman and Mills, 2001, p 79). In addition, "more than half the health information sites are owned by organisations likely to be biased or inaccurate" (Lenaghan, 1998, p 12). There have been reports of harm and even death directly attributable to information and advice individuals have obtained from some health websites (Duman and Mills, 2001, p 79). Clearly, poor health information can be conveyed through channels other than the Internet. Yet Duman and Mills draw attention to the exponential broadcasting factor of the medium, which means that the Internet can propagate poor quality or inaccurate information "far beyond its intended readership" (Duman and Mills, 2001, p 79).

Accordingly, health professionals have expressed concern about patients' reliance on unmediated self-access to Internet health information. Despite the direct involvement of health professionals in NHS Direct, clinicians and physicians have expressed strong concerns, feeling that it would undermine the role and gatekeeper function of GPs. Representatives of the British Medical Association (BMA) General Practitioner Committee predicted that the Internet 'would undermine the role of GPs and create inappropriate demand for services' (Pearce and Rosen, 2000, pp 54-5). However, this may also reflect an underlying anxiety relating to a perception of the undermining of the clinical autonomy of doctors. This notion of the 'deprofessionalisation' thesis was introduced in Chapter Two.

There needs to be support for health professionals' roles to "evolve and change … helping patients to navigate their way through complex and often contradictory information, rather than being the sole provider of information or care" (Kendall, 2000, p 21). UK health professionals can access such resources as the National Electronic Library for Health (NeLH) (see Box 7.1) and Organising Medical Networked Information, which is a gateway to evaluated, quality Internet resources in health and medicine (www.omni.ac.uk).

Health professionals can play a major role in supporting people "to have the skills and confidence to interpret and use new [Internet] mediums in a way that benefits them" (Kendall, 2000, p 21). Consulting NeLH – rather than what might be an out-of-date journal or book reference – can be both quicker and yield more accurate data. Additionally, studies have shown that "patients have significantly more confidence in doctors who look things up on a computer than in a textbook" (Johnson, 1988, cited in Wyatt, 1998, p 105).

In 1998, the then President of the General Medical Council, Sir Donald Irvine, stated that the doctor–patient relationship would strengthen in the Internet age, as doctors would be able to interpret the information for parents (Boseley, 1998). Five years later, this view was becoming the orthodoxy among many healthcare professionals. During an online debate on a BMA discussion document, the consensus answer of GPs to the question 'is the informed patient a threat or an opportunity?' was in the latter's favour. It was felt that GPs will

Box 7.1: National Electronic Library for Health

The National Electronic Library for Health (NeLH) has been conceived within the NHS as a virtual library that will act as an extensive online gateway to resources, including the National Institute of Clinical Excellence's guidelines to medical book reviews. The three core elements are 'knowledge and knowhow', bringing together research evidence and clinical guidelines; 'patient-focused information', including public health information on healthy lifestyles and community action to improve health; and 'learning opportunities', in terms of a virtual classroom for NHS professionals and staff. Newer developments have been the creation of virtual branch libraries within NeLH for the needs of particular professional areas (such as mental health, cancer), as well as peer support through online professional communities. The need for NeLH arose because it was increasingly difficult for medical professionals to keep abreast of developments even within their own specialties and to have access to a website in which they can have confidence in the quality of the information they are accessing. While "targeted primarily at healthcare professionals to support knowledge-based decision making, the site also provides patients and the public with access to the same information as their doctors and carers" (NeLH, 2003).

Sources: NeLH (2003); Weinberg (2001, pp 69-70); Abell and Oxbrow (2001, p 238); Fox (1998, p 30); NHSIA (2003)

have to become "even more of guides and translators of a mass of unfiltered information to help patients gain accurate knowledge" through putting information in the context of 'the big picture' (BMA, 2000). This was supported by a 2002 survey by the Health on the Net foundation, which found that 78% of health professionals agreed that patients' use of the Internet could make them more knowledgeable and facilitate communication between patients and professionals (Hughes et al, 2002, p 78).

Case study: social and housing workers

Information intermediaries are needed among sheltered housing and social services workers, for example, to help older people gain access to the Internet in order to benefit from online social welfare and leisure information. More specifically, a study of attitudes towards electronic service delivery in the area of social housing and social care found that many users felt the need for support by a professional information intermediary. Older people in sheltered housing, young people living in foyers and people with mental health problems all expressed concerns about having the necessary skills to complete service requests online. Their preferences were for more personal forms of interaction rather than "just an electronic form being sent to an unknown desk in an agency". They stressed that they often required the advocacy or communication support of a foyer worker or sheltered housing manager (Pleace and Quilgars, 2002, pp 44-5, 46, 53, 56).

While the information infrastructure in the social care sector is less developed than in the NHS, there is a web-based electronic library for social care (eLSC) that enables social care practitioners and managers to have access to the best available research and to have the tools to support evidence-based practice (NeLH, 2003).

Case study: community workers and volunteers

It is important, too, to consider the role of community information intermediaries. This type of support, based on the local needs of a community, might encompass face-to-face training and guidance of local people by volunteer workers, based on a physical infrastructure of PCs and perhaps supplemented by a peer support network.

In the US, workers and volunteers in community technology centres (CTCs) operate as information intermediaries for under-served minority and low-income Internet users, recognising that it is not sufficient for CTCs to provide computers and Internet connections. Community-based ICT centres within the concept of 'local nets' are discussed in Chapter Eight, as a model for reducing information exclusion.

Case study: librarians

Librarians traditionally seek to satisfy the information needs of library users and support the learning process. Public libraries, in the UK and internationally, now promote information literacy by offering Internet and PC access, and librarians have been developing new skills to provide guidance by passing on technical knowledge as well as the ability to evaluate content and information. The UK government has recognised the potential of a central role for libraries in providing "access to digital skills and services including e-government", which, in its 'new mission', sits alongside promoting reading and taking measures to tackle social exclusion (Safer Internet, 2003d; Department for Culture, Media and Sport, 2003).

Case study: family and friends

Finally, a potential category of information intermediaries that may be neglected by social welfare agencies is family and friends. Research by the National Family and Parenting Institute has found that while parents expressed mixed views about their experiences with professionals, "they consistently said that they turned to friends and family in preference to all other sources of information" (Keep, 2002, p 16).

Information intermediaries: an assessment

Most of those who work for organisations in whichever social welfare field are aware of a staff member who has access to technology and training but says that 'it's not for me'. An individual's awareness of the Internet – regardless of his or her technical *skills* – may not extend to knowledge of its 'availability, purpose, impact or benefits' (Greater London Authority et al, 2002, p 42). Therefore, they will be limited in acting as an information intermediary and also in ensuring that their organisation benefits from back-office integration of ICT systems (see Chapter Five). This experience is found, too, in the private sector, but sanctions will perhaps be more readily employed there. It seems reasonable to assume that job descriptions will shift to reflect these new functions.

In Chapter Eight, the vision of bringing about information inclusion will be explored through the UK's e-government policies. The main sociological groups – socioeconomic, spatial, disabled, and those defined by gender, age, race and ethnicity – will be revisited in the context of looking at how e-government initiatives may help overcome the digital divides set out in this chapter.

Thinklist

- **In accessing information from your workplace, what barriers do people face?**
- **Do you act as an information intermediary?**
- **Could you do this better?**

EIGHT

Where next? Social welfare practice and e-government

Introduction

In this chapter, the implications for social welfare of e-government and the criticisms levelled at UK e-government policy will be addressed.

In 2000, the editor of an Internet magazine set out a wish list of 'top-ten things I want to be able to do online', including:

- check the current waiting time at the local Accident & Emergency (A&E) department;
- be alerted to a webcast when my interests are being debated in parliament;
- see how many people have been prosecuted for driving while using a mobile phone;
- be told my passport's about to run out in time for me to be able to do something about it;
- get a maths A-level;
- apply for housing benefit;
- find my national insurance number;
- complain to my MP and get a reply the same day;
- see whether more police or traffic wardens patrol my street;
- vote (Kreisky, 2000, p xxiv).

Depending exactly on where he now lives in the UK, this editor would find only four out of 10 of these applications possible in 2003.

This chapter will examine:

- Who is e-government for – the government to save costs or citizens for greater convenience and accessibility?
- What are the obstacles to e-government, including online transactions in social welfare services?
- What are the implications for social welfare professionals' practice and agencies' service provision?

E-government in the UK

The vision

E-government can be defined as "the provision and organisation of public services through new electronic channels" (Curthoys and Crabtree, 2003, p 9).

From the mid- to late 1990s, the consensus among ICT commentators and politicians was that societal trends would ensure that access to Internet technologies was going to increase exponentially, via:

- increasing levels of PC home ownership and rising computer literacy within the household;
- development of more user-friendly, multimedia technology, including interactive digital TV;
- new generations being more at ease with ICT;
- Internet access becoming increasingly available in the public and voluntary sectors, as well as in the high street;
- more accessible gateways to government information, starting to be configured around 'life episodes' (like health, employment) rather than bureaucratic silos that reflect government departments (Prime Minister and Minister for the Cabinet Office, 1999).

Implementation

In 1997, the UK government set the target of all government services being available electronically to everyone who wants it by 2008. In March 2000, this was revised to bring the target forward to 2005. Subsequently, the 2005 target has been extended to local government, so that all local authorities, since 2001, must produce their own 'Implementing electronic government' statements (Office of the e-Envoy, 2002).

By 'available', the government meant both a 'geographical component' and "a component of knowledge and capability to utilise the technology" (*New Statesman*, 2000, p xix). This can be understood as meaning that *not* everyone should have access, but that anyone should who desires it, from any socioeconomic group, of any gender, age or race. Therefore, the crucial interrelationship between 'socioeconomic circumstances' and physical *access* and 'socio-personal barriers' of *skills* is recognised, as set out in Chapter Seven (Greater London Authority et al, 2002, p 13).

The key influence on the e-government vision clearly derives from e-commerce. Indeed, the 'digital divide' issues examined in Chapter Seven show that information access barriers for socially excluded groups may apply as *equally* to online shopping as to social welfare services.

Carrots and sticks

The guiding principle of e-government in the UK continues to be to "streamline the collection and sharing of data [in order to make] ... services more accessible, and reduce social exclusion", and reduce cost (Prime Minister and Minister for the Cabinet Office, 2000). It is no secret that cost efficiencies are intrinsic to the design and implementation of e-government policies. In a pamphlet produced in 1997, an influential policy analyst held out the hope that such automation as electronic one-stop shops would yield staff cost savings to the tune of approximately £3.5 billion. Alongside the economic benefits to government, the convenience for people of not having to be in liaison with so many agencies, and the ICT potential of more customised or individualised public services would mean that "service levels too could be transformed" (Byrne, 1997, pp 9, 17, 18, 24-5).

Again, e-government is not simply about computers. Electronic service delivery may be through digital television channels, websites, mobile technology, the telephone and smartcards. The way the individual experiences the ICT-delivered information or service may also be indirect, through professionals or staff in call centres or at counter services in, say, one-stop shops. The Office of the e-Envoy was created in the Cabinet Office to steer the roll-out of e-government. Initial focus has been on 'quick wins' of providing online options for more straightforward public service transactions, including passport applications and tax returns.

In the private sector, banking or insurance firms, for example, can both encourage customers to use automated and online interaction (carrots) and penalise those who prefer to remain using more traditional forms of delivery (sticks). A bank can offer higher interest rates for online banking, charge for transactions in person or even by phone and ultimately close branches. However, despite its monopolistic or near-monopolistic position in public service provision, the government has few 'sticks', and must, therefore, develop and employ a range of 'carrots', including:

- establishing public access points for widespread Internet use, through different types of kiosk technology and digital interactive television;
- access and training initiatives, for example, community-based schemes, including 'Wired Up Communities' for promoting ICT usage.

The story of kiosks

Kiosks originated as touch-screen computers, like bank ATM cashpoints, which operate by prompting the user to touch the area on the screen that links to the desired information. Locations were planned outside social security offices, in bus stations and supermarkets, and were designed to appeal to potential Internet users who were without access at work or home. The scheme has developed in the UK as a public and private sector partnership, which launched the country's first free outdoor e-mail service, *Freemail*.

From spring 2001, a new scheme by the government and Mothercare saw in-store childcare information kiosks being set up that contain information from the user-friendly *ChildcareLink* interactive website (www.childcarelink.gov.uk). In 2001, pilot schemes in post offices began to offer an advice service and the opportunity to interact with the Inland Revenue, local authorities, voluntary bodies and commercial providers; but this was discontinued in October 2002 (Comptroller and Auditor General, 2003, p 6). The Jobcentre Plus Employment Service introduced touchscreen kiosks in jobcentres, as well as in supermarkets and even pubs, in 2002, while that year also saw British Telecom's variant of the kiosk concept in the implementation of a new Internet-capable Multiphone in streets, stations and shopping centres.

Digital interactive television

"The breakthrough for internet shopping will come when the internet is accessed through the living room television set" (Hampson, 2000, p 3). This was the received wisdom in 2000 for e-commerce and is important in relation to social welfare usage.

The new technology of digital interactive television (DITV), launched in the UK at the end of 1998, can offer higher sound and picture quality than analogue TV. It also makes it possible to deliver many more channels and programme services, including localised content and video on demand. When combined with a telephone line it can provide interactive services, including e-mail, text messaging, voting, home banking and interactive entertainment. In essence, DITV paves the way for 'one-way broadcasting' to become 'two-way interactive communication', both for leisure and public services purposes (Smith and Webster, 2002, p 25).

By offering the same, core functions of ICT, DITV has the potential to become the PC of the future. Since it "uses a familiar technology [television] in a convenient location [living-room]" (Smith and Webster, 2002, p 32), it has the advantage of being a more user-friendly medium than the PC for interactivity, whether for booking holidays or for finding health advice on NHS Direct Online. Many non-PC users have acquired interactivity familiarity by using Teletext. In January 2002, MORI data showed that 44% of UK adults had DITV at home, while surveys since 2000 have been indicating that PC ownership is likely to tail off at around 50% of households in the UK. Although its penetration is lowest among low-income households, data from Oftel and the Office for National Statistics (ONS) confirm that the difference in usage between DE, AB and C social grades is far less pronounced than with home Internet access (Hughes et al, 2002, p 24).

Accordingly, e-government policy has placed much emphasis on the view that there is extensive scope for DITV to "become a significant 'electronic' service-delivery channel for public service providers" (Smith and Webster, 2002, p 26). In spring 2002, a DITV pilot service was launched to provide UK online content (www.ukonline.gov.uk) as well as introducing an interactive television access point to its ChildcareLink national telephone helpline and website, using the UpMyStreet local information search directory (Cabinet Office, 2002b; DfES, 2002). Department of Health DITV trials (with four cable channels) also piloted healthcare information and advice, though evaluation found that they reached no more than 30% of potential viewers (*Future Health Bulletin*, 2003a). It is envisaged that this initial phase of DITV information placement will provide the basis for "viewers to conduct online transactions in areas such as health, education and social services" (Cabinet Office, 2002b). This is based on envisaging that, by 2006, more than three quarters of UK homes will have digital television (Cabinet Office, 2002a).

As will be set out shortly, however, the key criterion for further take-up of DITV will be "the development of compelling content and activities that will stimulate service use and demand" (Smith and Webster, 2002, p 32).

Community-based ICT resource centres

At the early stages of the Internet's development, it was recognised that support and training needed to be included in public access schemes. This would enable Internet and computer novices to gain the basic knowledge and confidence to develop their interactive use of the PC platform for public services as well as leisure purposes. Additionally, central to local government – and statutory agency to voluntary sector – support would be vital for developing the physical infrastructure in order for community-based resource centres to function effectively as grass-roots, public-access points to the Internet. A second 'carrot' was to develop community ICT facilities (see Box 8.1).

In their original conception, community-based ICT centres were to:

- act as hubs of various kinds of community activity;
- generate communication across and within the community, not just siphering information from centralised agencies;
- provide access to local service information, as well as offer channels for local consultation;
- act as a locus for people to acquire communication and information-handling ICT skills; and
- offer significant opportunities for community groups and small non-governmental organisations to publish information (National Working Party on Social Inclusion, 1997, pp 46-7).

Two models of community-based ICT centres that developed in the UK were 'cybercafés' and 'telecottages'. Cybercafés became a feature of urban areas by the late 1990s, as multi-functional, high-street venues that typically offer chargeable Internet access alongside café facilities. The rural equivalent was 'telecottages', often within the voluntary sector, attracting public sector support and offering subsidised training and Internet access (*Internet Intelligence Bulletin*, 1999a). By way of helping community groups acquire an online presence, some local authorities have developed community websites that provide an infrastructure for local groups to register details of their services and activities (for example, see www.brent.gov.uk/brain). Websites and regional organisations, such as lasa, provide guidance on using volunteers for community IT projects (Lasa Information Systems Team, 2003; www.it4communities.org.uk). Evaluations of this approach have been extremely positive (Hellawell, 2001). These projects empower users to both find and then develop for themselves "relevant and owned content" (Harvey, 2002, p 9).

The parallel evolution, alongside (physical) community-based ICT centres, of 'local nets' and community networking will be discussed in the context of e-democracy in Chapter Nine.

Box 8.1: Wired Up Communities

A pilot programme by the UK government (2000-03) – Wired Up Communities – installed computers in homes and schools in areas of high social deprivation across England. The aim was to bridge the digital divide by providing free equipment for Internet access, alongside training and a specially designed website highlighting access to learning and employment opportunities. The original pilot in Kensington, Liverpool, was launched in February 2001, aiming to install 2,000 computers during that year. Six further pilot projects were selected in March 2001, reflecting a variety of technological (PC or set-top box) and spatial (urban, rural, coalfield) characteristics. Independent evaluation in 2003 found that Wired Up Communities made a major contribution to helping residents to bridge a key aspect of the digital divide: 59% of respondents used the Internet at home for the first time and almost half reported using it daily. Yet more than a quarter (26%) had not used the hardware to access the Internet, split between those who said they lacked skills and those who lacked the interest. Fewer than two in 10 Internet users had sought information about, or sought to communicate with, a range of local community-based and local organisations. The Wired Up Communities initiative has been terminated and there are no plans to extend it. Its website does provide a practitioner's tool-kit, however, as a guide to planning, setting up and running a community-based ICT project.

Sources: DfEE (2001); DfES (2003b); www.dfes.gov.uk/wired/

Content, content, content

> The three most important criteria for producing a successful Web site are content, content and content. (Mansfield, 1997, p 56)

Whether kiosk schemes, DITV, community-based ICT centres and 'Wired Up Communities' schemes succeed in narrowing the 'digital divide' critically depends on *content*. *Access* and *skills* acquisition is a means to an end, the end being the 'right' information produced for citizens by the Internet and other ICT platforms.

Examination of the socioeconomic and geographic dimensions was presented earlier. The issue of content relates directly to gender, age, disability and ethnicity (see Box 8.2).

Bridging the digital divide

Realising rights and citizenship

As was outlined in Chapter Two, ICT has the potential to "reinforce and strengthen the rights of all by providing instant access to a wide range of public information, entertainment, retail, education and health services" (Chester, 1998). For some commentators, although there are only two million connections in the UK (at May 2003), broadband technology for accessing the Internet has been described as acting as "an infrastructure of emancipation" (Kearns, 2002, p 51).

The motivation factor

Yet innovation has to be accompanied by recognition of the benefits of ICT by citizens. Put simply, "those that have crossed the digital divide have found reasons to do so" (Servon, 2002, p 11). A summer 2003 survey by the Oxford Internet Institute found that 41% of Britons aged 14 and over do not use the Internet: of these non-users, 44% were 'indifferent', 17% were 'passive', 17% identified as 'refuseniks' and 22% were 'proxy users', using friends and family as information intermediaries to send an e-mail or for e-commerce (*Economist*, 2003, p 43).

An essential link between content and usage is *motivation*. For social welfare service users and professionals alike, information inclusion requires the belief that ICT is useful to their, or their clients' welfare, as well as to meet other educational and leisure needs. Physical access and skills training are necessary but not sufficient conditions to bridging the digital divide.

As a recent research study concluded, in order to ensure that "socio-personal barriers [of] attitudinal and behavioural factors" are addressed, issues of "levels of interest, awareness, understanding and acceptance of ICTs" must be made the priority for government at all levels (Greater London Authority et al, 2002, p 11). Indeed, an important motivating element may be provided through greater ICT familiarisation with online voting when interacting with the latest quiz, talent or reality TV shows, such as *Big Brother*. Others, who are perhaps less socially excluded and further 'down the line' in seeing the benefits of ICT, are already using DITV or websites directly to access public and welfare services. A September 2002 UK Online questionnaire found that 67% of site users would be 'very or quite likely to apply for a passport on interactive TV', yet

Box 8.2: Content and gender, age, disability and ethnicity

In gender terms, an innovative element in the implementation of the Mayor's Londonwide Domestic Violence Strategy has been the development of a 'Domestic Violence Channel' on the *i-plus* kiosk network. These are Internet kiosks (there are 65 across London) located indoors and outdoors, in shopping areas and at transport hubs, which provide free information. Crucially, women in abusive and violent relationships can, when perpetrators are not present, access the kiosks completely anonymously (Greater London Authority, 2002; Mayor of London, 2002; Editorial, 2001, p 7).

For older people, IT 2 Eat is a local initiative (based in Rotherham, South Yorkshire) providing flexible access opportunities for older people to use the Internet. It provides IT equipment, support and information and advice on diet and health to local people over 55 with mobility problems. The scheme gives otherwise isolated older people the opportunity both to shop and research their genealogy online, as well as providing nutritional advice by a community dietician from the local primary care trust (Miller, 2002, pp 32-3). At the other end of the age range, The Site (a Youthnet project, www.thesite.org) illustrates the role of a young person's website in providing non-stigmatising and self-referral information and advice on a range of welfare, health and relationship issues.

Respond is a website and telephone helpline (0808 808 0700) to help people with learning disabilities who have been sexually or physically abused. In 2001, it was found that fewer than 205 of the 1,103 calls to the helpline were from people with learning disabilities; most of the users were carers, relatives and professionals. In response, a new website section was designed, to appeal to the increasing number of people with mild learning disabilities who have Internet access. The next phase of development (2002-05) is to use a community fund grant to increase accessibility for those with severe learning disabilities (Pring, 2002, pp 127-8; www.respond.org.uk).

Finally, Black Information Link (BLINK) was set up by the 1990 Trust in 1997 to address the information-technology disadvantage of black and minority ethnic (BME) communities in the UK and the lack of relevant online content. The aim was to provide up-to-date information on health, education, personal finance, community services, IT, race equality policies and black arts and entertainment. For example, *BLINK*'s 'healthweb' offers a searchable database on all illnesses and conditions affecting BME communities, with signposting to further information, resources and expertise (Adams, 1997, pp 27-8; SEU, 1998, p 5; www.blink.org.uk).

only half reported that they mostly used the UK Online interactive service (on Sky digital TV) for information – fewer than for games (36%) or for shopping (13%) (Cabinet Office, 2002b).

The Oxford Institute Report has concluded that it would take "a generation or more before nine-tenths of Britons regularly use the Internet", due to the lack of interest. Its radical thesis is that, since many users are happy to remain 'offline' even when access is available, this indicates that 'not using the Internet is a lifestyle choice, not a form of social deprivation'. Hence, there is a 'digital choice' as well as a 'digital divide' between users and non-users' (*Economist*, 2003, p 43).

Citizen choice

Previous chapters have emphasised that ICT is one method of managing and communicating information. While ICT does not offer complete solutions to information exclusion, it should be recognised too that all other forms of accessing information have built-in problems. It is just that people are so used to them that they do not recognise them when they occur.

Figure 8.1, in a simplified way, shows that letters present barriers to those with low levels of literacy, as well as to the blind and visually impaired. Face-to-face customer service or professionals' support can be inaccessible to those with mobility problems through disability and age, and to those who may feel stigmatised in directly accessing social welfare (especially social) services. The standard telephone is not suited to the deaf and, at the extremes of social exclusion, to those too poor to have a telephone.

The implication for e-government is that ICT must be seen as supplementary to, *not a substitute for*, other forms of 'first contact' for social welfare services, whether in person, by phone or through printed material (see Chapter Three). There must be choice of channel, so that, for example, the benefits of accessing instant and current information via intranets and the Internet via information intermediaries at an advice bureau or health centre can still be realised (see Chapter Seven).

Figure 8.1: Problems of accessing information across different mediums

Information/service channel	Exclusion
Letter	Illiterate, blind
Phone	Deaf, poor, non-English speaker
Face to face	Non-mobile, stigmatised, non-English speaker
Internet	Poor, unskilled, uninterested

Source: adapted from Leabeater (1998)

Chapter Two described concerns about ensuring confidentiality and security of information by social welfare professionals, service users and citizens, and how they can be overcome (for example, by encryption). In terms of social welfare data – especially given the imperative for greater inter-agency information sharing (see Chapter Five) – government agencies need, too, to demonstrate the security of communication channels and privacy to the public's and professionals' satisfaction. A lack of confidence in either group will lead to lack of usage.

The curve of normal distribution

ICT strategy, as we saw in Chapter Three, must form part of, and be subsidiary to, the organisation's information management strategy. ICT applications at the user interface – and between organisations – need to be complementary to other forms of information and service provision, as has been emphasised throughout this and earlier chapters. The requirement for relevant content and providing *motivation* sits alongside *access* and *skills* factors, and constitutes an essential dimension to the task of addressing the digital divide (see Curthoys and Crabtree, 2003, pp 33-5).

The curve of normal distribution (in Figure 8.2) illustrates these different dimensions. At the start of the curve, there is a small but significant number of the digitally excluded, for whom *access, skills* and *motivation* are low and hence who are still in need of greater support and encouragement to use ICT. These individuals are the target of government schemes to engage those who have not yet experienced any benefits of going online, such as 'Get Started' (2003), which offered free Internet starter sessions at over 6,000 venues across the UK (Office of the e-Envoy, 2003a). Similarly, in the London Borough of Newham, a choice-based lettings initiative empowers people on the housing register to use touch-screen terminals installed in local libraries and community centres (or a telephone hotline) in order to find a property that meets their needs from a list posted on the website in 10 community languages (www.ellchpoicehomes.org.uk; Clapperton, 2003, p 10).

There is a key role to be played by community information intermediaries to encourage socially and ICT-excluded groups to move further along 'the curve'. The development of different content for different groups is vital.

The increasingly largest cohort (the peak of the curve) comprises those people who, through perhaps e-mail, the Internet or DITV at work and home (and, if adults, through their children), can and do use ICT to access mainstream government services. Many would be receptive to this channel offering interactive social welfare services, such as directly booking hospital appointments online.

Lastly, as the curve falls, there is a much smaller number of people with high levels of ICT access, skills and motivation. Their income and education levels support the first two factors, while their professional concerns are likely to greatly aid their motivation.

Figure 8.2: The curve of normal distribution

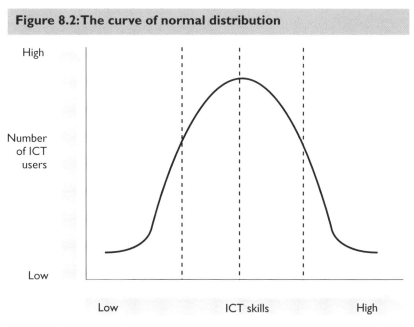

	ICT skills		
	Low	Medium	High
Motivation	Low: Need support and encouragement	Medium: Build in incentives. Market	High: Minimum incentives needed
Access to ICT equipment	Low: Ensure access to hardware and software at wide variety of locations with easy-to-access support	Medium: Used for other activities eg games, interactive TV	High: In office, at home and increasingly on the move
Skills	Low: Need Wired Up Communities' taster sessions, support and training	Medium: Systems need to be straightforward and reliable	Can have complex ICT systems with minimal support
Category	Digitally excluded/ margins of exclusion	Mainstream. Universal services	Professional services
Examples	Wired Up Communities	£10 discount for tax return online	Land Registry

For example, a solicitor or surveyor will have a strong incentive to use the National Land Information Service for online land searches in conveyancing work. Thus, nearly 40% of local authorities in England and Wales now offer an equivalent or lower price for electronic searches (Powell, 2003).

Problems with e-government policies

At the start of this decade, "lots of information, but precious little interaction" (Kreisky, 2000, p xxii) characterised public services websites in the UK. This was sufficient for, say, submitting electronic tax return forms but not functional for transactional social welfare services (see Chapter Four). Nevertheless, in an e-government study, Accenture rated the UK in the second highest tier of 'maturity' as a country with government portals offering strong online services. Only Canada had reached the highest tier of 'service transformation', with government services available through 'multiple delivery channels' and offering information access to the public via audience, subject, department and agency routes. At the same time, 77% of Canadians surveyed felt that the Internet would improve the way they received services from government (Accenture, 2003 p 6).

By 2003, only 10 council websites in the UK could be classed as 'transactional'; the facility for electronic transactions was rare for NHS trust websites; and many GP surgeries and health centres did not even have a website (Mathieson, 2003, p 19). However, at a national level the UK government launched its first major online transactional social welfare service in 2002 – a facility to claim child benefit through the Internet. However, is this for the benefit of the agency or the user? A Department for Work and Pensions (DWP) survey of public attitudes towards the use of electronic benefit services found that while around 50% of its clients had some knowledge of technology, some 30% had never used a computer. When informed of the possibilities for online services, only around half said they would be likely to use the Internet to contact the DWP (*E-Government Bulletin*, 2002). By 2005, the normal method of paying benefits and tax credits will be through direct payment into claimants' bank or post office card accounts – yet some disabled people and those with mental health problems, for example, may have difficulties remembering PINs or operating ATMs (Edwards, 2003, p 6).

Particularly in low-income areas, more than just access is required: "there is an issue of engagement with the mind, of motivation and incentive, as well as access" (*New Statesman*, 2000, p xx). Foley and Alfonso criticise what they see as a technocratic approach of UK e-government practice – that is, as if all that is required is access to the technology since everyone will use it. They draw upon research showing that a growing number of non-users believe they have 'no need' for the Internet – as well as the nine million non-users who declare a 'lack of interest' in the technology – to conclude that, unless non-users are convinced that ICT has some advantages, they will not be tempted to use free public online access points. Nor will they attempt to budget for their own PC or other platform for the Internet (Foley and Alfonso, 2002).

As far back as 1998, when people were asked about how they would wish to use DITV, independent market research found that public service activities scored 'distinctly higher' than commercial activities. Compared with 41% favouring home banking and 26% online shopping, 48% sought better access to government services – including 61% for medical advice, 36% for social services advice and 52% for information on education and training (*Government Computing*, 1998, p 13). In 2002, in an ONS survey, fewer than 20% of UK adult Internet users said that they used it to access government services, compared with 28% for financial services online and 74% for searching for information about goods and services (Greater London Authority et al, 2002, p 35). While there cannot be any direct data comparison, the wide difference does suggest that the there is now greater motivation for e-commerce than e-government, at least among current users. This is likely to indicate the under-development of e-government services and their marketing to those currently using the Internet, let alone those at the excluded end of the 'digital divide' spectrum.

An assessment of the progress of e-government (in 2003) can usefully be made against a benchmark of the characteristics of a socially inclusive information society (of the mid-1990s):

- ready, easy-to-use public and individual access to the communication channels;
- information that is essential for full participation in society available at no cost at the point of delivery; and
- heavy investment in the information-handling and communication skills of citizens, which raise their levels of information awareness and ability to exploit information (National Working Party on Social Inclusion, 1997, p 9).

If we take all three criteria together, there has been some progress but not sufficient to overcome a 'digital divide' based on accessibility, skills, content and motivation. Kiosks have not proved popular, undermining the public access-point model. After all, if you go to the kiosk you might as well go to the local office. CTCs and Wired Up Communities have reached only small proportions of the information excluded. If the need (in rights and equity terms) is for universal access in everyone's home, then, while the absolute cost of the hardware and Internet access charges has diminished, costs remain significantly high while the motivation levels have not been correspondingly raised.

Ultimately, e-government policy has not yet 'squared the circle' of usage and provision in the UK: only "when sufficient socially excluded users are online will usage approach a threshold that encourages the provision of more information and services for socially excluded groups" (Greater London Authority et al, 2002, p 60).

Future prospects

Equity in universal access?

In 2000, the then UK government Minister for Learning and Technology questioned whether commercial providers would offer "the full upstream and downstream capacity you need to get the full advantage of the internet in an educational sense on digital TV". This was contrasted with the dedicated, educational resource of a PC-based platform for the Internet more likely to exist in higher-income households (*New Statesman*, 2000, p xvi). Similarly,

Castells warns that the future heralds more "price-based differentiation" in delivery and that "the scope of Internet-based inequality" may be extended in terms of speed of connection, level of interactivity and flexibility of use across platforms (Castells, 2001, pp 257-8). A two-tier system might well be developing, by which only 'premier' Internet users will gain access to the full range of public service content (see Box 8.3).

This underscores the earlier discussion, in Chapter Two, of the central role of social rights and citizenship in social welfare. For Tambini, universal Internet rights of access are defined as:

> ... not only rights for all citizens, but also rights to easy access without hindrance to the entire universe of cultural goods that digital communications media offer, including free public content and government services. (Tambini, 2000b, p 18)

His thesis is "the idea of a citizen's right to access digital services, rights not only to connectivity, but also content" (Tambini, 2000b, p 5). Moreover, when such a right to online access exists, "a public authority [should] ... be called upon to deliver on a citizen's claim to an entitlement". While he recognises that such rights do depend on resources, he invokes the pragmatic argument that "the economy will benefit from a connected citizenry" (Tambini, 2000b, p 19). Tambini warns that "the Internet should be about access to almost infinite content, not a selection of carefully chosen interactive services" (Tambini, 2000a, p vii).

Box 8.3: A two-tier system?

In government–business partnerships, for online channels in the 'mass market' – in cable and digital television – only certain public information and services may be made available. While the proliferation of DITV and kiosks as enabling channels for the Internet can help to widen (physical) access, it may not bring greater access to content. Kiosks are designed to simplify access to and navigation of the 'raw' Internet by providing a restricted platform of a touch-screen format. Most (Microsoft) Word and PDF files cannot be accessed through DITV. Accordingly, kiosk and DITV users are limited in their ability to read many online resources of public health information and engage in more interactive, social welfare processes.

Sources: Ticher and Powell (2000, p 134); Bellamy and Bolsover (2001); Hughes et al (2002, p 100)

Future trends

Four trends can be identified:

- People's self-access to support and advocacy via ICT has become a significant trend and is likely to accelerate. The model is simple: parents access a website devoted to dyslexia, for example. They discover a new chat-room feature through which they learn of the experiences of other families. They may meet in a geographical locality to campaign for better local services. In turn, this is likely to make them more prepared to have an online relationship with professionals when formal service provision is required.
- Current policy developments in UK social welfare services and e-government is likely to both influence and be influenced by the growing erosion of formal service boundaries. The trend towards portals, with 'lifestyle' or 'life-time episodes', parallels the structural and attitudinal changes resulting from the political and professional recognition that vertical 'silos' of healthcare, social care and other welfare functions often fail to improve outcomes for users. For example, in the Green Paper, *Every child matters*, this is illustrated by the integrated approach of information, referral and tracking systems and the longer-term aim of single children's departments across social services, health and education (DfES, 2003a). Therefore, social welfare professionals' willingness to embrace an 'information intermediary' role across different areas may be enhanced by these 'macro' developments in the same direction of integrated information and services across agencies.
- E-government developments will increasingly need to reflect the requirements of closer European integration. The European Union (EU), with its minimal internal borders, will mean that, in terms of public administration, "citizenship must be something more closely tied to a person than their place of birth" (Farhi Zihni, president of the local government IT management body, *Socitm*). Accordingly, at local and central government levels, a more mobile European population will need ICT systems that are integrated across the EU – just as they are across agencies within individual states – in order to deliver online benefits, pensions or taxation transactions (Parkinson, 2003a).
- Government now must balance this promotion of online usage by children and young people with taking action to safeguard against children's online access to unsuitable material (see Chapter Two for fuller discussion). This dual message is promoted to parents via www.parentsonline.gov.uk and, in 2002-03, the UK government ran a major 'safer surfing' awareness campaign and initiated legislation on a specific 'grooming' offence on the Internet (2003 Sexual Offences Act). The campaign provided clear messages to children (and parents) that they should never give out personal contact details online, and never meet with someone they have met online unless accompanied by an adult (Home Office, 2003). Such government action was a response to children's charities' lobbying and parental concerns: in a

2001 Hansard Society public survey, "making the Internet safe for children" was respondents' first preference for the government's e-government priority (HM Government, 2002, p 13).

The UK government has placed the development of e-government at the centre of its modernising government agenda since the mid-1990s, particularly from 1997 onwards. Nevertheless, while the e-government programme has sought to transform 'the process of change [in public services] driven by the ICT revolution', Peter Hennessy (1999, p 4) reminds us that, while the government may have embraced ICT, it 'cannot accurately predict let alone steer' its future course.

Clearly, e-government is not a passing fad of politicians, public service managers and ICT experts. A number of public service transactions are now operable online. However, as well as needing to pilot the technology required, online social welfare transactions in more complex, multi-agency areas of social welfare have yet to be properly embraced – by both professionals (as information intermediaries and direct users of back/front-office integrated ICT systems – see Chapters Five and Seven) and the public (in access, skills and motivation terms).

In Chapter Nine, final consideration will be given to ICT for social welfare through the significance of ICT and democracy for citizens. This will be outlined in the wider context of issues of convergence, dissent and control and different models of technology.

Thinklist

- **How is e-government affecting you?**
- **Where would your service users be on the curve of normal distribution? Is this changing?**
- **Is the content you provide actually what people want?**

NINE

Where next? Social welfare practice and emerging technology

Introduction

This chapter puts social welfare practice in the wider context of:

- the politicians who shape social welfare practice through legislation and policy;
- the current and future role of ICT in the democratic process;
- the role of ICT in developing and supporting the whole community;
- the use of ICT by the voluntary sector in campaigning for change;
- the potential risk of ICT in terms of the invasion of privacy and excessive government control.

It goes on to explore what the future might hold and translates this into practice for social welfare practitioners.

Democracy is the foundation of social welfare, and elected politicians are pivotal in this process – so it makes sense to start with politicians and their likely perspectives on ICT.

Politicians and ICT

A recurring theme of this book has been the lessons that can be drawn from societal responses to new technologies. One conclusion is that politicians like to be associated with new technology. Victorian politicians identified themselves with the growth of the railway (Hardy, 2003). A century later, Harold Wilson is remembered for his 'white heat of technology' speech:

> ... Wilson, summoned Labour to embrace the cult of the new and to harness the white heat of the technological revolution.... There was no room in the Labour movement for Luddites or antique working practices. (MacArthur, 1993, p 336)

A similar situation has developed between New Labour and ICT:

> Given that New Labour is obsessed with 'modernisation' ever since its emergence as a political force, it was inevitable that it would find the Internet

irresistible. And so it proved, with Downing St and the Cabinet Office pumping out windy phrases about making Britain the most 'e-friendly' country in the world, the appointment of an 'e-envoy' and a deluge of hooey composed by picking words and adding the 'e-' prefix as in 'eGovernment', 'eLearning', 'eDemocracy' ... 'Britain', gushed Blair, 'has the potential to become a technological powerhouse'. (Naughton, 2002)

The concept of the 'certainty trough' was introduced in Chapter Six. This model described the idea that 'a little knowledge is a dangerous thing'. It seems likely, then, that for the immediate future – despite the scale of the problems described in Chapter Six – ICT will continue to be seen as a panacea for managing the problems of social welfare.

Democracy, participation and ICT

Given this, it is perhaps inevitable that ICT will also be seen as a means for reinvigorating active citizenship and democracy. For many, ICT "holds the key to the enhancement of the democratic aspects of the political process and to the creation of new opportunities for citizen participation" (Bryan et al, 1998, p 2).

The idea is as follows. The most direct form of democracy is that of the public forum; where people come together to talk and to decide on the matters that concern them, without any of the troublesome intermediaries of representative politicians, the media, pressure groups and advertising. This is a view reflected in the title 'Back to Greece' (Adonis and Mulgan, 1997). This can be seen as another manifestation of the idea of 'transactional glue' introduced in Chapter One. The complexities of modern processes mean that we are bound together – but also 'tied up' – by the actions of all these intermediaries. In contrast, ICT cuts through all this – it has a disintermediating effect (see Chapter One) – allowing potentially direct access to the political processes.

The main elements of this can be identified as follows:

- Relevant, timely information is key to communal decision making. ICT can deliver this information.
- Public feedback improves political decision making. ICT can put people in touch with politicians.
- Public space is essential for people to meet and decide. The Internet provides a space where all can meet virtually.
- Dialogue should be central to the political process. ICT allows people to initiate and inform this process (see, for example, Bryan et al, 1998, pp 5-7).

Might this make a difference in practice? A good indicator might be the UK government portal UK Online, which gives access to a range of government services via the web (see Chapter Five). A function of the portal was to enhance democracy by promoting public debate on public services on the Internet.

However, a six-month survey by the Institute of Public Policy Research (IPPR) found that the forum Citizen Space was used mostly by a small number of people, with short postings of 'ill-informed opinion, prejudice and abuse'. The IPPR concluded that this low level and poor quality of usage was linked to the fact that Citizen Space "lacked a clear purpose or connection to government policy making" (Hirst, 2003, p 6). But surely the users of Citizen Space bear some responsibility to? As Korac-Kakabadse and Korac-Kakabadse (1999, p 218) argue, ICT might provide the tools but "it does not provide time or ability or inclination".

At a higher level of participation, Blumer and Coleman (2001) suggest the idea of 'a civic commons in cyberspace', an attempt to create an electronic forum where issues of common importance can be learned about and discussed. The forum should not be simply a talking shop but an integral part of the decision-making process:

> Each year the Chancellor of the Exchequer produces a pre-budget consultation paper which is read and responded to by a relatively narrow range of people in the City. It would be useful to open up this process of consultation, utilising digital TV perhaps to invite the public to respond to policy options and discuss ways that their localities or professions would be affected by particular decisions. (Blumer and Coleman, 2001, p 20)

No doubt, this would be useful to a few. But the phenomenon of information overload (see Chapter Three) will surely mean that this level of detail is one step too far, even for most dedicated welfare policy analyst. An instructive historical parallel might be the introduction of televising proceedings in Parliament, initially of the two Houses and subsequently select committees as well. Televising these proceedings must qualify as progress since political processes have become more transparent. But it is doubtful how many people have actually taken the opportunity to watch these proceedings. While any attempt to further open up the processes of government and policy making is welcome, it is difficult to avoid the conclusion that even under the best circumstances such a model would serve only a tiny minority of the population.

Meanwhile, actual participation in the electoral process in the UK is, of course, continuing to fall:

> The UK came only 65th, for example, out of 163 countries, when ranked according to average turnout in national elections between 1990 and 1997. And, as we all know, UK national turnout slumped even further to an appallingly low figure of only 59.4% in the 2001 General Election ... the situation in local government is even worse than it is at national level. Local government elections saw a 29.6% turnout in 2000, falling from an average 41% in the 20 years between 1976 and 1996. This situation comes perilously close to removing the claim of any local authority to speak with legitimacy as the authentic voice of its community. (Kearns et al, 2002, p 13)

'E-democracy' is: "the use of ICT in support of citizen-centred democratic processes" (Kearns et al, 2002, p 12). In specific terms, e-democracy might include the following:

- the use of e-voting techniques to create technologies to create possible plebiscitary or direct democracy;
- the use of online techniques to sample public opinion (for example, through online polls;
- the building of online communities by local community groups (see Chapter Eight); and
- the use of website discussion spaces and e-mail discussion groups to stimulate online public deliberation and debate (Kearns et al, 2002, p 12).

Does e-democracy actually work? ICT clearly does play some role in encouraging and sustaining electoral activity. For example, an 80-year-old father of a friend who had been severely disabled by a series of strokes was able to participate in the local election via SMS voting. Thus, Kearns et al (2002) cite *Election 2001: The official results*:

> In the post election survey conducted by MORI for the electoral commission, 21% of non-voters said they had not voted because it was too inconvenient to get to the polling station, while a further 16% of non-voters gave being away on election day as the main reason for not taking part. (Electoral Commission, 2001)

However, is low voting turnout entirely due to difficulties in getting to the polls? Given the relentless downward trend in electoral participation, the temptation must be to think other factors are at play. Indeed, a report in *The Guardian* suggested just this. In relation to e-voting (via SMS, website or kiosk), it stated:

> ... the evidence gathered so far paints a very mixed picture. In its evaluation of the smaller-scale e-voting trials run in areas such as Sheffield and Liverpool last year, the electoral commission, a government voting watchdog concluded: 'The pilots appear to have provided a vital building block in establishing public confidence. However, the evidence in relation to turnout remains unconvincing at this stage'. (Parker, 2003)

Swindon went for the DITV (digital, hence interactive TV) route of e-voting. *The Guardian* reported that turnout rose by 3.5%; better than before – but hardly a ringing endorsement of a revitalised model of democracy.

The suspicion must be that most of the people who use the new channels would have voted anyway and so these models ease the process for existing participants without encouraging non-voters (see, for example, Cross, 2003b).

In Chapter Six, the idea was introduced that the application of ICT will help satisfactory or good organisations perform better, but it would not solve the problems of a struggling organisation. If there are fundamental problems with electoral participation in the UK, then ICT alone will not solve them. One conclusion might be that in supporting active democracy ICT is necessary but not sufficient. But politics is not the sole preserve of politicians and governments and it is this wider field that is now explored.

Communities and ICT

Civic society can be conceived of as the intermediate 'layer' between individuals and the state and comprises the voluntary sector, faith organisations, unions, professional groups, formal and informal groups, clubs and societies (see, for example, Prochaska, 2002). Civic society is a key locus for social capital – the concept introduced in Chapter Two and defined as "the features of social organisations such as networks, norms and social trust that facilitate coordination and cooperation for mutual benefit" (Putnam, 2000, p 229).

Community networking and local nets are the ICT-enabled versions of civic society. They can operate at the level of particular housing estates such as Redbricks in Manchester, towns such as Blacksburg (Kavanaugh and Paterson, 2002) or indeed cities such as Amsterdam's De Digitale Stad (Castells, 2001). As Hick and McNutt (2002, p 12) put it: "Community networks, or FreeNets, are locality based systems designed to serve their immediate communities with ways to communicate and deliberate virtually".

Chapter One introduced the idea that new technologies are absorbed into our normal routines of life. In this model, these 'virtual communities' live alongside existing communities, supplementing them rather than supplanting them. Just as civic society provides 'schools of citizenship' (see, for example, Prochaska, 2002) so these ICT-enabled civic societies can enable democracy and citizen participation too. For social welfare purposes, these facilities have a real practical purpose: "Community information networks are the online equivalent of cards in the corner shop window; they enable local people to find or supply information about health, jobs, services, training and leisure" (MacGillivray and Boyle, 2001, p 125).

It makes sense for practitioners to work with the grain of these community networks and local nets, not only those that exist already but also those that will emerge in the next few years. Indeed, some practitioners will want to help establish them. There is a parallel with the virtual support communities described in Chapter Four: work with such groups referring individuals to them, supporting those that provide them and where needs require if establishing partnerships to deliver them.

Campaigns and social change

But "[c]ommunities do not simply organise themselves.... Organising requires people. Someone must build strong enough relationships between individuals that they support each other through long struggles for social change – and if the community already exists, someone must help it to support social action" (McNutt and Hick, 2002, p 73).

Jubilee 2000 was a global campaign to link debt alleviation for developing countries with the celebration of the millennium:

> In 1996, Jubilee 2000 had the backing of three UK Church Aid Agencies and about 180 individual supporters.... In less than four years time, Jubilee 2000 was set up in more than sixty countries, had won the backing of tens of thousands of organisations and had handed more than 24 million petition signatures to the leading creditor nations. (Buxton, 2002, p 130)

Part of the strength of Jubilee 2000 was to link both communities of interest (see Chapter One) such as churches, faith groups, political groups, unions and professional groups with geographical communities across the developing nations; in short, linking physical networks with electronic networks. As Buxton puts it, the reason

> ... the Internet played such a crucial role is that its structure as a system of networked computers fitted closely with Jubilee 2000's central strategy of reaching networks and individuals who could pass the campaign message on to larger networks. (Buxton, 2002, p 132)

A gigantic virtual community had come about – a community that wanted to end debt.

This process of major social change being leveraged through the convergence of social and electronic networks is not just restricted to the voluntary sector (see Box 9.1).

ICT can put 'media power' – once the exclusive preserve of large private companies – into the hands of small voluntary sector groups. As Saxton and Game put it:

> For most charities that want to communicate a message to a mass audience, the traditional choice has been between paying for an advertising campaign or hoping that the media will publicise a particular issue. An advertising campaign needs deep pockets, and effective media coverage usually means relinquishing control of your message to newspaper journalists and TV reporters. The Internet provides a mass communications tool which does not rely on intermediaries and costs a fraction of an advertising campaign. This puts the power to communicate back in the hands of charities and away from those who all too often don't share the same perspective.... (Saxton and Game, 2001, p 5)

Box 9.1: Texting the revolution

An article in the *Independent* about political campaigning in the Philippines contrasted the political revolution that overthrew the dictator Ferdinand Marcos in 1986 with the revolution that overthrew President Estrada in 2001:

> Organising any national movement is a vast undertaking in the
> Philippines, an archipelago of 7,100 islands, 2,000 of them inhabited
> and many of them suffering from wretched communication.

That was until the advent of the mobile phone. Despite the poverty of the country, 4.5 million people have mobile phones. Filipinos send 52 million text messages a day – 11 for every mobile phone owner. Calls cannot easily be traced because most telephones are 'pay-as-you-go'. In short, texting is an ideal way to organise a revolution. The article described the mobilisation of a mass demonstration by texting. As one organiser commented: "In revolutions people used to say, 'Keep your powder dry'". Now they say, 'Keep your cellphone charged'"

Source: Parry (2001)

Convergence

The ability to move content between channels, and increasingly the affordability of so doing (see Chapter Three), means that the power of the image (symbol, photograph, film) and sound (music, recording), once the preserve of the mass media, is now available to the smallest groups. A voluntary sector group can shoot a film on a digital camcorder, use it in a staff presentation, paste it on the website and e-mail it to anywhere in the world. This ability to move content between channels can be described as 'convergence'. A strict definition of convergence might be that:

> ... [d]igital technology allows all forms of information to be recorded,
> processed and distributed in a common electronic form. (Dutton, 2001,
> p 71)

However, at a broader level, the concept of convergence can provide a useful conceptual shorthand for understanding the wider impact of ICT. There is also convergence between "the once separate technologies and industries of print, broadcasting and telecommunications" (Dutton, 2001, p 87) and a corresponding convergence at an organisational level: for example, the merger between Time Warner (best known for film and TV productions) and AOL (an internet service provider).

'Infotainment' (introduced in Chapter One) is the convergence of entertainment and, in this case, social welfare material. A good example is www.thesite.org.uk, which combines entertainment with objective advice for young people about drugs, crime, sexually transmitted disease and contraception. Perhaps 'infotainment' will become increasingly predominant in the practice of social welfare.

There is also a convergence between the mass media and politics: "The center of the new political system appears to be the media" (McLeod et al, 1994). Thus, Rupert Murdoch has been assiduously courted by New Labour because of his control of many media outlets in the UK. Silvio Berlusconi, Prime Minister of Italy, and Michael Bloomberg, Mayor of New York, are both heads of large media conglomerates. At a more prosaic level, as media channels proliferate with ever smaller audiences ('narrow casting'), politicians need ever greater help from a range of media professionals to get their message across (Blumer and Coleman, 2001).

For those involved in campaign and communication work – whether in the voluntary sector or the public sector – the use of image and sound via ICT will increase. As Buxton argues: "... future campaigns will be unable to ignore the vehicle of the Internet and still be successful" (Buxton, 2002, p 140). However, as this book has continually emphasised, this technology can complement but it cannot substitute for other elements of campaign and communication. If this is the positive impact of ICT on social change, it has a downside as well.

Dissent and control

On 23 May 2003, *The Guardian* reported the government's proposals to introduce an identity card:

> Under Mr Blunkett's proposal, the card is expected to carry name, date of birth, address, employment status, sex, photo, national insurance, passport and driving licence numbers, and a password or PIN to authorise transactions. It will also carry 'biometric information' such as an eye scan or electronic fingerprint to guard against identity fraud. Everybody will be required to register for the new national database but it will not be compulsory to carry the card.... (*The Guardian*, 2003)

The card is being promoted as an 'entitlement' card to claim benefits, medical care and so forth; no card, no service. At the time of writing, the precise timescale for introduction of the card is uncertain. *The Guardian* reported on 7 November 2003 (Wintour, 2003b) that technological preparations would go ahead on a national entitlement card with a view to roll-out in 10 years' time; however, contrary to expectations, these proposals were not included in the Queen's speech opening Parliament that month.

Chapter Eight introduced the idea of the public being able to access services online. To access services electronically, there needs to be a foolproof system for certifying one's personal identity. In this light, entitlement cards – or ID cards – are not simply a gimmick or a means of excluding certain groups (for example, illegal migrants) from services. They are an essential part of public service delivery. Kearns puts it like this:

> ... there is a clear trend toward rolling out technologies ... and smart cards which will provide much stronger identification of individuals when they are engaged in activities online. They also can be used as the basis for far greater personalisation of service either from government or business. However, while bringing these benefits, digital certificates and smart cards also create the potential both for greater state monitoring of individuals and for increasingly individualised assessments of consumer risk. The former represents a potentially significant shift of power away from the individual and toward the state. (Kearns, 2002, p 5)

To what extent do electronic ID cards represent a shift to the surveillance state or is this simply an Orwellian fantasy? Richard Thomas (the Information Commissioner, the role replacing that of Data Protection Registrar), interviewed on the entitlement cards "told BBC Radio 4's *Today* programme: 'I do have anxieties about a monolithic state system having so much information on every single citizen in this country'" (Morris, 2003).

As has been shown, ICT has the potential to develop communities. It also has the potential to undermine privacy, increase state control and undermine other rights that perhaps are taken for granted. The Royal Society of Arts states:

> There is a paradox here. By increasing connectivity and networking ICT can raise social capital – the key ingredient of sustainable development. But if people's private information is held by a greater number of authorities or corporations (a development clearly promoted by ICT), it could decrease peoples' trust in government and politics and, as a consequence, social capital could diminish. (Jervis, 2002)

There are, of course, important legal safeguards in place in the UK: the 1998 Data Protection Act, the 2000 Freedom of Information Act and the 1998 Human Rights Act (see Chapter Two). But perhaps a surveillance society would be more likely to come about via incrementalism than by conscious decision and systematic roll-out; a gradual linking of databases across government departments and a linking of individuals with data in the database. Previous chapters have described how 'joined-up' government was not simply a metaphor; it was a process of coalescing information resources across the public domains. The increasing shift to swipe cards (for example, with driving licences and compulsory bank cards) and eventually ID cards could be seen as part of this development. Some of the possible linkages are perhaps surprising (see Box 9.2).

Box 9.2: The world your Oyster?

Transport for London has recently introduced a new smartcard system, Oyster. Credit card-sized cards replace tickets and are used to activate ticket barriers. A card contains personal details and can be 'charged' online. It is possible to monitor travel patterns of specific cardholders. Unusual patterns can be flagged by monitoring systems. So it might be possible to track a missing young person, or it would allow all children to be monitored who were out after 9pm. Schools might be interested if use was during school hours and so forth. Presumably, the movements of adult individuals known to the authorities could be tracked too.

Source: Transport for London (2003)

A further step is the linking of information in the public domain with information in the private domain. Information management is routinely supplied to the government by private providers. A process described as APNR shows the potential of linking public and private domains (see Box 9.3).

Public and private

The increasing convergence between the public and private sectors is nothing new. Indeed the Home Secretary, in the 2003 Edith Kahn Memorial Lecture, was able to pose the rhetorical question, apparently without irony: "Who should own ... public services ...?" (Blunkett, 2003, p 20). ICT projects are routinely outsourced (see, for example, *Computing*, 2003).

In Chapter One, the historical development of the Internet was described and it was explained how it was brought about by a combination of state, public and private activities. Most software development today is in the hands of the private sector. The source code is the private property of the developer. Technology is often seen as 'value neutral'; but if, as this book has argued, ICT is the product of people, its creators' values will be embedded in it (Kearns, 2002). Kearns illustrates this with a telling example.

Box 9.3: Public and private?

ANPR stands for Automatic Number Plate Recognition. Roadside scanners operated by the police (the public domain) read 3,500 number plates per hour, checking them against other public domain databases to determine whether vehicles are licensed or belong to a individual wanted by the police. However, ANPR also uses private domain databases – it checks to see whether cars are insured by drawing on car insurers' databases (private domain) (Puttnam, 2003). (For a comprehensive overview, see Graham and Wood, 2003.)

With the software provided by his Internet service provider (ISP – the organisation that links computers to the web), Kearns can contact people with like-minded political views, develop ideas and actions with them, and broadcast the results and organise accordingly. Using the software, he can become a member of any such group in the world, whether legitimate or not. There is one exception. He cannot contact the fellow users of his ISP *as a group*. Why is this? The software does not allow it. He concludes that this is because the commercial provider of the software does not want to run the risk of creating a ready-made lobby that might take a collective view about its commercial provider (Kearns, 2002).

Again, an historical analogy. Dutton (2001) describes the Napoleonic messaging system in France. Moveable arms relayed signals between towers. In 1844 over 500 towers fanned out from Paris to reach 27 cities: "its design enabled the central authorities to communicate easily with the provinces at the same time that it made it difficult for the provinces to communicate among themselves" (Dutton, 2001, p 63).

As Kearns asks, how comfortable should we be that the values of the codes are exclusively in private hands? Further, this is not a model that has to be lived with – there are other ways. Software is available that has 'open source' code. Open source has been defined as: "when a user may obtain a copy at no cost, study its source code, modify it and distribute it to other users for free" (Leadbeater, 2003, p 24). Linux is one such open source operating system. (For a more detailed sociological perspective see Castells, 2001.) The 'open source' movement shares important values with the culture of social welfare (see, for example Goetz, 2003). For example, in social welfare, it is unusual for good ideas to be defined as intellectual property, copyrighted and then sold. Rather, whether at the practitioner, professional or organisational level, good ideas are shared – to be used free of charge by others and, it is to be hoped, further improved in turn.

What might this mean in terms of ICT for social welfare managers? Well, the London Borough of Newham has decided to migrate to Linux (*The Guardian*, 2003c, p 2). The municipality of Munich has decided to switch its 14,000 PCs from Microsoft to Linux. The municipality of Lower Saxony has followed suit. As a result, the German Interior Ministry had to switch to Linux for its police and security services. This was not simply about savings, but as Interior Minister Otto Schily said: "We are raising computer security by avoiding a monoculture and we are lowering dependence on a single supplier. And so we are a leader in creating more diversity in the computer field" (Naughton, 2003b).

Consumer or citizen?

In Chapter Two, the issue of citizen versus consumer was introduced. A citizen is an active player in society. "It is through helping others, taking responsibility, and making decisions that the citizen is formed ..." (Mulgan, 1998, p 122). In this model, the individual's claims to healthcare, education and so forth are predicated on citizenship, but they comprise only a small part of what is a more expansive concept. In contrast, the consumer has a narrow transactional relationship with suppliers, whether the market, the state, or the market funded by the state (see, for example, Williams, 2002).

John Hudson (2003) argues that debates about the *delivery* of ICT (the consumerist model) are increasingly taking over from more important concerns about social welfare generally (the citizenship model) (see also Curthoys and Crabtree, 2003). He characterises the consumerist model as 'e-galitarianism', in which the debate about the role of ICT in the delivery of services and the consequent hyperbole have drowned out a concern about social justice and inequality. In contrast, 'e-egalitarianism' is a genuine concern with the issues of citizenship and community, which relegates technical issues about ICT to their subordinate – but rightful – place. Kearns develops this idea further: "... the Government ... is ... heavily focused on the transactions performable over the network rather than on what the nature of the network itself ought to be". The values of ICT can be positive. ICT "... can be used creatively to extend the range of opportunities available for active citizenship. And it can be used to deepen and to extend a commitment to the liberal state, which itself provides the space within which an equal and active citizenry can exist"(Kearns, 2002, p 4).

Implications

What are the implications of all this for social welfare practice and management? Predicting the future is always difficult. But on this analysis, seven trends seem to emerge.

*   ICT as a central mechanism for the delivery of public services is here to stay and will grow in influence despite the negative experiences and setbacks of the kind catalogued in Chapter Six.
*   E-democracy will develop in a manner that is complementary to other forms of democratic participation (such as meetings, consultations, the ballot box) but by itself will not resolve the problems of low participation in the democratic process.
*   Those in social welfare must work with the grain of virtual communities of support as well as emerging community nets and local networks. This should translate into formal recognition and incorporation into organisational IMS and ICT strategies as well as being reflected in day-to-day practice.
*   The power of multimedia will become increasingly important in delivering services. 'Infotainment' in practice (if not in name) will become increasingly important in delivering social welfare objectives.
*   The extent to which the voluntary sector and campaign groups understand and adopt ICT as 'necessary but not sufficient' will define whether their campaigns for change are successful.

- Entitlement cards seem to be firmly on the political agenda. The integration of public and voluntary agencies by virtual means will give this form of identification increasing importance. Without a radical change of policy, entitlement cards will become embedded in day-to-day work.
- Managers, practitioners and professionals in social welfare are citizens too. The extent to which they shape the emerging social welfare services of the future will reflect not just their role as employees but the extent to which they are – or become – active citizens.

Thinklist

- **How might you draw on ICT-enabled support groups, campaign groups and community nets in delivering your work objectives?**
- **How might your work involve a range of media (for example, film, sound, imagery) in delivering your work objectives?**
- **What would the entitlement card mean for your work?**

Thinklist

The 'you' in the thinklist questions is deliberately ambiguous: it can be applied to individual practice, to practice within the team or to senior management teams looking at organisation-wide functions, or even to the whole organisation. There are no 'pat' answers; rather, the questions are designed to encourage engagement with the issues.

Chapter One

- What resources (time, energy, money) do you invest in ICT?
- Has this gone up, down, or stayed the same over the past five years?
- What has been positive about this? What has been negative?

Chapter Two

- How important is information in the provision of your services?
- The 1998 Data Protection Act is frequently misunderstood. What are the main principles underlying the Act (see www.informationcommissioner.gov.uk)? Should you change your practice?
- What is the range of mechanisms to protect children, and adults, from exposure to offensive material and potential dangers of abuse on the Internet?

Chapter Three

- What knowledge does your work require you to have?
- Categorise this knowledge: is it tacit or explicit, informal or formal?
- Is this how it should be?

Chapter Four

- What are your main flows of information?
- Do you have an information management strategy?
- What might this mean for the three 'C's: content, channel, communication?

Chapter Five

• What is your information chain? Where are the breaks and duplications?
• What is the information chain between your front office and back office; between your workplace and partner agencies; over your agency and your partner agencies?
• How could this be improved?

Chapter Six

• The funding of ICT: what model are you experiencing?
• How inclusive is your ICT planning, development and delivery?
• Do you have an ICT strategy?

Chapter Seven

• In accessing information from your workplace, what barriers do people face?
• Do you act as an information intermediary?
• Could you do this better?

Chapter Eight

• How is e-government affecting you?
• Where would your service users be on the curve of normal distribution? Is this changing?
• Is the content you provide actually what people want?

Chapter Nine

• How might you draw on ICT-enabled support groups, campaign groups and community nets in delivering your work objectives?
• How might your work involve a range of media in delivering your work objectives (for example, film, sound, imagery)?
• What would the entitlement card mean for your work?

Bibliography

Abell, A. and Oxbrow, N. (2001) *Competing with knowledge: The information professional in the knowledge management age*, London: Library Association Publishing.

Adams, R. (1996) *Social work and empowerment*, London: Macmillan.

Adams, J. (1997) 'Black information link: using IT to support minority communities', *Assignation*, vol 14, no 4.

Adonis, A. and Mulgan, G. (1997) 'Back to Greece', in G. Mulgan (ed) *Life after politics: New thinking for the twenty-first century*, London: Fontana, pp 227-45.

Ahituv, N. and Neumann, S. (1987) 'Decision making and the value of information', in R. Galliers (ed) *Information analysis: Selected readings*, London: Addison Wesley.

Alexander, D. (2003) 'The ties that bind', *Progress*, June/July, pp 26-7.

Arete Software Ltd (2003) *Functional specification of the interaction between the PLR and LAS systems for the Pan London Register*, London: Arete.

Arnold, J. and Turley, S. (1996) *Accounting for management decisions*, London: Prentice Hall.

Ashcroft, C., Kartallozi, N. and McQuillan, D. (2003) 'Language net', *lasa computanews*, issue 127, October, pp 6-7.

Atkinson. D. (1999) *Advocacy: A review*, Brighton/York: Pavilion Publishing/ Joseph Rowntree Foundation.

Audit Commission (1994) *High risk/high potential: A management handbook on information technology in local government*, London: HMSO.

Audit Commission (2002) *Data remember: Improving the quality of patient base information in the NHS*, London: Audit Commission.

Audit Commission and SSI (Social Services Inspectorate) (1996) *Joint review of social services functions*, London: Audit Commission/SSI.

Ballantine, J. and Cunningham, N. (1999) 'Strategic information systems planning', in R. Heeks (ed) *Reinventing government in the information age*, London: Routledge, pp 293-311.

Bamford, T. (1996) 'Information driven decision-making: fact or fantasy?', in A. Kerslake and N. Gould (eds) *Information management in social services*, Aldershot: Ashgate, pp 18-28.

Bateman, N. (2000) *Advocacy skills for health and social care professionals*, London: Jessica Kingsley.

Batty, D. (2003) 'File not found', *Guardian Society*, 29 October, p 10.

Baudrillard, J. (1988) *America*, London: Verso.

Baudrillard, J. (2000) *Sumulcra and simulation*, Ann Arbor, MI: University of Michigan Press.

Bawden, D. (2001) 'Information overload', *Library and information briefings*, Issue 92, January.

Bayliss, V. (2003) *Redefining work 2*, London: Royal Society of Arts and Accenture.

BBC News (2001) 'US breaks child cyber-porn ring' (http://news.bbc.co.uk/1/hi/world/americas/1481253.stm, accessed 18 November 2003).

Bellamy, C. and Taylor, J. (1998) 'Governing in the information age', in R. Heeks (ed) *Reinventing government in the information age*, London: Routledge.

Bellamy, K. and Bolsover, J (2001) 'Chatroom Sheffield shows the world how to do public internet access', *Local Government Chronicle*, 7 September, p 20.

Blumer, J. and Coleman, S. (2001) *Realising democracy online: A civic commons in cyberspace*, Research Publication No 1, London: Institute of Public Policy Research/Citizens Online.

Blunkett, D. (2003) 'Civil renewal: a new agenda', The CSV Edith Kahn Memorial Lecture, 11 June, London: Home Office/CSV.

British Medical Association (2000) 'Shaping tomorrow: issues facing general practice in the new millennium', online discussion (www.bma.org.uk, accessed 12 March).

Bowcott, O. (2003) 'Curbs on chat: grooming to be outlawed', *The Guardian*, 15 July.

BBC News (2002a) 'Parents alerted to safe surfing benefits' (www.bbc.co.uk, accessed 20 November).

BBC News (2002b) Report on *Today*, BBC Radio 4, 13 December, 8.00am.

BBC News (2003) Report on *Today*, BBC Radio 4, 10 February, 7.15am.

Brake, D. (2002) 'Beyond government', *E-government Bulletin*, no 122, 20 September (www.headstar.com/egb/).

Broadbent, J. and Laughlin, R. (1997) 'Contracts, competition and accounting in health and education', in S. Deakin and J. Michie (eds) *Contracts, co-operation and competition*, Oxford: Oxford University Press.

Brooks, F., Macintyre, M., Scott, P., Quick, K. and Taplin, D. (2001) 'Reshaping health professionals' communication', in E. Carson, F. Harvey and M. Hughes (eds) *eHealth: a futurescope – Proceedings of the 3rd International conference on advances in the delivery of healthcare*, 4-6 April, City University London, London: City University, pp 63-8.

Brown, J. and Duguid, P. (2002) *The social life of information*, Boston, MA: Harvard Business School Publishing.

Browne, A. (2000) 'GPs to prescribe drugs by email', *Observer*, 10 September.

Bryan, C., Tsagarousianou, R. and Tambini, D. (1998) 'Electronic democracy and the civic networking movement', in R. Tsagarousianou, D. Tambini, and C. Bryan (eds) *Cyberdemocracy technology, cities and civic networks*, London: Routledge, pp 1-17.

Buxton, N. (2002) 'Dial up networking: a case study of Jubilee 2000', in S. Hick and J. McNutt (eds) *Advocacy, activism and the internet: Community organisation and social policy*, Chicago, IL: Lyceum, pp 129-42.

Byrne, L. (1997) *Information age government: Delivering the Blair revolution*, London: Fabian Society.

Byrne, P. (2001) 'I can see clearly now the website's changed', *Local Government Chronicle*, 12 October, p 20.

Cabinet Office (2000) 'e.Gov: electronic government services for the 21st century' (www.cabinet-office.gov.uk/innovation/reports/reports.shtml, accessed 28 April 2003).

Cabinet Office (2002a) 'Access ability – with UK online interactive', Press Notice CAB 046/02, London: Cabinet Office, 10 April.

Cabinet Office (2002b) 'Public say yes to UK online interactive', Press Notice CAB 182/02, London: Cabinet Office, 10 September.

Cairncross, F. (2001) *The death of distance 2.0*, London: TEXERE Publishing.

Caldow, J. (2002) 'Seven e-government milestones', in E. Milner (ed) *Delivering the vision: Public services for the information society and the knowledge economy*, London and New York, NY: Routledge, pp 17-38.

Canaan, C. (1992) *Changing families, changing welfare: Family centres and the welfare state*, London: Harvester Wheatsheaf.

Capeling, N. (2002) 'Fame and fortune', *Charity Times*, December, pp 54-5.

Carter, R. (2003) 'Microsoft chatrooms to close after abuse fear', *The Guardian*, 24 September, p 1.

Castells, M. (2001) *The Internet galaxy: Reflections on the Internet, business and society*, Oxford: Oxford University Press.

Castells, M. and Himanen, P. (2003) *The information society and the welfare state: The Finnish model*, Oxford: Oxford University Press.

Chancellor of the Duchy of Lancaster and Cabinet Minister for Public Service (1997) *The government's response to comments on the Green Paper government.direct*, London: The Stationery Office.

Chatterjee, M. (2002) 'Claims to fame', *Housing Today*, 21 November, pp 30-2.

Chester, J. (1998) *Towards a human information society*, European Union ACTS Programme, USINACTS Project, Loughborough: European Union.

Children and Young People's Unit (2002) *Local preventive strategy – Draft guidance*, London: CYPU.

Clapperton, G. (2003) 'The gold standard', *epublic: Guardian Society*, 8 October, p 10.

Clark, C. (2000) 'Only IT can realise the promise of joint working', *Community Care*, 19-25 October, p 13.

Cohen, D. (2003) 'Revolution?: it's all go on the western front', *Guardian Money*, 8 February, pp 14-15.

Coleman, J. (1988) 'Social capital is the creation of human capital', *American Journal of Sociology*, vol 94, supplement S95-S120.

Comptroller and Auditor General (2003) *Progress in making e-services accessible to all – Encouraging use by older people*, Report by the Comptroller and Auditor General HC 428, 20 February, London: The Stationery Office.

Computing (2003) 'US company to manage NHS IT programme', 27 March, p 1.

Cooper, H., Arber, S., Fee, L. and Ginn, J. (1999) *The influence of social support and social capital on health*, London: Health Education Authority.

Craig, Y. (1998a) 'Introduction', in Y. Craig (ed) *Advocacy, counselling and mediation in casework*, London: Jessica Kingsley, pp 11-22.

Craig, Y. (1998b) 'Conclusion', in Y. Craig (ed) *Advocacy, counselling and mediation in casework*, London: Jessica Kingsley, pp 237-42.

Crick, B. (2000) 'The Citizenship Order for schools', in N. Pearce and J. Hallgarten (eds) *Tomorrow's citizens?*, London: Institute of Public Policy Research, pp 77-83.

Cross, M. (2000) 'Lives online', *Guardian Society*, 15 November, pp 2-3.

Cross, M. (2003a) 'Internet cuts the red tape' (http://politics.guardian.co.uk, 20 February, accessed 24 March).

Cross, M. (2003b) 'Poll position', *epublic: Guardian Society*, 8 October, p 8.

Cross, M. (2003c) 'Eyes on the child', *The Guardian*, 19 September.

Crystal, D. (1997) *The Cambridge encyclopedia of the English language*, Cambridge: Cambridge University Press.

Curthoys, N. and Crabtree, J. (2003) *Smartgov: Renewing electronic government for improved service delivery*, London: The Work Foundation.

Daft, R. and Lengel, R. (nd) 'Organizational information requirements, media richness and structural design', *Management Science*, vol 32, no 5, cited in R. Heeks (ed) (1999) *Reinventing government in the information age*, London: Routledge, pp 554-71.

Daniels, C. (1994) *Information technology: The management challenge*, Wokingham: Addison-Wesley/The Economist Intelligence Unit.

Davies, C. (1997) 'The information infrastructure approach for developing countries', Paper presented at 'Public Sector Management in the Next Century' Conference, 29 June-2 July, University of Manchester, cited in R. Heeks (ed) *Reinventing government in the information age*, London: Routledge.

Deloitte Research (2001) *Through the portal: Enterprise transformation for e-government*, London: Deloitte Consulting/Deloitte & Touche.

Department of Constitutional Affairs (2003) 'Data sharing in the public sector: guidance on the law' (www.dca.gov.uk/foi/sharing/toolkit/coveringletter.htm, accessed 27 November).

Department for Culture, Media and Sport (2003) 'Libraries, learning and information in the next decade' (www.culture.gov.uk, accessed 28 May).

DfEE (Department for Education and Employment) (1997) *Connecting the learning society*, London: DfEE.

DfEE (1998) *The learning age*, London: DfEE, p 13, cited in P. Jarvis (2002) 'Active citizenship and the learning society', *LLinE (Lifelong Learning in Europe)*, vol 1, KVS Foundation/Finnish Adult Education Research Society: Helsinki, Finland, p 22.

DfEE (2000) 'Preparing your application', *Wired communities application pack*, London: DfEE, pp 42-8.

DfEE (2001) '12,000 homes to get wired up in £10m programme', Press Notice 2001/0142, 16 March.

DfES (Department for Education and Skills) (2001) 'Virtually all schools are now connected to the Internet – Ashton', Press Notice 2002/0334, London: DfES, 4 September.

DfES (2002) 'Ashton launches first national government interactive TV service', Press Notice 2002/0078, London: DfES, 18 April.

DfES (2003a) *Every child matters*, London: DfES.

DfES (2003b) *Connecting communities to the Internet: Evaluation of the Wired Up Communities Programme*, Research Brief No 389, London: DfES.

Digital Home (2003) 'Straight outta Compton St', *Digital Home*, Issue 3, August, p 26.

DoH (Department of Health) (1995) *Child protection: Messages from research*, London: HMSO.

DoH (1997) *The new NHS*, White Paper, Cm 3807, London: The Stationery Office.

DoH (2002) 'Delivering 21st century IT support to the NHS: national specification for integrated care records service – consultation draft', Executive Summary (www.doh.gov.uk, accessed 28 May 2003).

DoH (2003) 'NHS Direct to more than double in size', Press Release 2003/ 0165, 15 April.

DoH/SSI (2003) 'Better informed? SSI national inspection report of the management and use of information in social care' (www.doh.gov.uk/ssi/ betterinformed.htm, accessed 30 May), pp 1, 24, 29-31.

DoH (Department of Health) and Welsh Assembly Government (2003) 'Information outputs for children's services', Consultation draft (www.doh.gov.uk, accessed 30 May).

Drury, C. (1996) *Management and cost accounting* (4th edn), London: International Thompson Business Press.

DTI (Department of Trade and Industry) (2000) *Closing the digital divide: Information and communication technologies in deprived areas*, Report by Policy Action Team 15, London: DTI.

DTI (2003a) 'New wave broadband', Press Release P/2003/048, London: DTI, 28 January.

DTI (2003b) 'Britain gets connected', Press Release P/2003/426, 31 July, London: DTI.

Ducatel, K., Webster, J. and Hermann, W. (2000a) 'Information infrastructures or societies', in K. Ducatel, J. Webster and W. Hermann (eds) *The information society in Europe: Work and life in an age of globalisation*, Oxford: Rowan and Littlefield, pp 1-17.

Ducatel, K., Shapiro, H., Rees, T. and Weinkopf, C. (2000b) 'Towards the learning labour market', in K. Ducatel, J. Webster and W. Hermann (eds) *The information society in Europe: Work and life in an age of globalisation*, Oxford: Rowan and Littlefield, pp 141-71.

Duman, M. and Mills, P. (2001) 'Consumer health information: but what about me?', in E. Carson, F. Harvey and M. Hughes (eds) *eHealth: a futurescope – Proceedings of the 3rd International Conference on Advances in the Delivery of Healthcare*, 4-6 April, City University London, London: City University, pp 79-80.

Dutton, W. (ed) (1996) *Information and communication technologies: Visions and realities*, Oxford: Oxford University Press.

Dutton, W. (ed) (2001) *Society on the line: Information politics in the digital age*, Oxford: Oxford University Press.

Dyson, J. (1994) *Accounting for non-accounting students* (3rd edn), London: Pitman Publishing.

E-Access Bulletin (2003) 'Brent Browsealoud', issue 46, October (www.e-accessibility.com).

Earl, M. (1989) *Management strategies for information technology*, London: Prentice-Hall.

Economist (1998) 'Paradox lost', in 'Going digital: how new technology is changing our lives', London: The Economist.

Economist (2003) 'The digital divide: Internet? No thanks', 20 September.

Edwards, C., Ward, J. and Blytheway, A. (1995) *The essence of information systems* (2nd edn), Hemel Hempstead: Prentice-Hall.

Edwards, S. (2003) 'Without exception', *Evidence*, October, London: Citizens' Advice Bureau, pp 6-7.

E-Government Bulletin (2002) 'No fanfare for child benefit online', issue 125, 8 November (www.headstar.com/egb/).

E-Government Bulletin (2003a) 'Welwyn Hatfield sees it right', issue 130, 7 February (www.headstar.com/egb/).

E-Government Bulletin (2003b) 'Spring "soft launch" for government store', issue 146, 3 October (www.headstar.com/egb/).

E-Government Bulletin (2003c) 'Housing estate in wireless experiment', issue 145, 19 September (www.headstar.com/egb/).

Electoral Commission (2001) *Election 2001: The official results*, London: Politicus.

Elston, M. (1991) 'The politics of professional power: medicine in a changing health service', in J. Gabe et al (eds) *The sociology of the health services*, London: Routledge.

Ericson, R. and Haggerty, K. (2001) 'Electronic policing', in A. Giddens (ed) *Sociology: Introductory readings*, London: Polity.

Eriksen, T. (2003) *Tyranny of the moment: Fast and slow time in the information age*, London: Pluto Press.

ESRI (2003) 'CRM and GIS at Tower Hamlets' (www.electronic-government.com/esri, accessed 8 May).

Evans, P. and Wurster, T. (2000) *Blown to bits: How the new economics of information transforms strategy*, Boston, MA: Harvard Business School Press.

Fitzpatrick, T. (2003) 'Introduction: new technologies and social policy', *Critical Social Theory*, vol 23, no 2, pp 131-8.

Fletcher, T. (2002) 'Talk the talk', *E-Government Bulletin*, no 118, 22 July (www.headstar.com/egb/).

Foley, P. and Alfonso, X. (2002) 'Lack of access – or lack of interest?', *E-Government Bulletin,* no 123, 11 October (www.headstar.com/egb/).

Fox, J. (1998) 'Computers, decision making and clinical effectiveness', in J. Lenaghan (ed) *Rethinking IT and health*, London: Institute of Public Policy Research, pp 30-54.

Future Health Bulletin (2003a) 'Digital television trials a mixed success', issue 16, February (www.headstar.com/futurehealth).

Future Health Bulletin (2003b) 'Personal "healthspace" for NHS Direct Online', issue 17, March/April (www.headstar.com/futurehealth).

Gann, B. (2000) 'Empowering the patient and public through information technology', in J. Lenaghan (ed) *Rethinking IT and health*, London: Institute of Public Policy Research, pp 123-39.

Garret, P. (2003) 'The daring experiment: the London County Council and the discharge from care of children to Ireland in the 1950s and 1960s', *Journal of Social Policy*, vol 32, no 1, January 2003, pp 75-91

Gartner Group cited in D. Morley, M. Maybury and B. Thuraisingham (eds) (2002) *Knowledge management: Classic and contemporary works*, Cambridge, MA: MIT Press, p xii.

Giddens, A. (2001) 'The scope of sociology', in A. Giddens (ed) *Sociology: Introductory readings*, London: Polity, pp 3-6.

Giddens, A. (2002) *Sociology*, London: Polity.

Gilchrist, A. (2000) *Community development and networking*, London: Standing Conference on Community Development/Community Development Foundation.

Gill, T. (1996) *Electronic children: How children are responding to the information revolution*, London: National Children's Bureau.

Gillen, S. (2003) 'Fears grow that Haringey social services are still failing children', *Community Care*, 16-22 October.

Giller, H. (1996) 'Monitoring for effective management in social services', in A. Kerslake and N. Gould (eds) *Information management in social services*, Aldershot: Ashgate, pp 36-47.

Global Consulting UK Ltd (2003) *Scoping the availability of software in ethnic minority languages within the UK*, DfES-Commissioned Research Report No 387, London: DfES.

Goetz, T. (2003) 'Open source software everywhere: software is just the beginning...', *Wired Magazine*, November, pp 158-208.

Gold, S. (2003) 'The digital dilemma of the NHS', *epublic: Guardian Society*, 8 October, p 23.

Gould, N. (2003) 'The caring professions and information technology: in search of a theory', in E. Harlow and S. Webb (eds) *Information and communication technologies in the welfare services*, London: Jessica Kingsley, pp 29-48.

Government Computing (1998) 'TV view', *Government Computing*, January, p 13.

Graham, S. and Wood, D. (2003) 'Digitalizing surveillance: categorisation, space, inequality, *Critical Social Policy*, vol 23, no 2.

Greater London Authority (2002) 'Digital domestic violence resource used by 5,000 in first 25 days', News Release GLA/2002/199, 25 April.

Greater London Authority, London Development Agency and LondonConnects (2002) *The digital divide in a world city*, London: GLA.

Greenwood, M. (2003) 'Electronic public information', Paper delivered to 15th Annual Conference of the Society of Public Information Networks (SPIN) on Electronic Public Information 2003, 22 May, Birmingham.

Griffin, C. (1998) 'Down your way', *Local Government Management*, Winter, pp 14-15.

Guardian, The (2003) 'Government faces £1.5 billion bill for IT failures', 12 March 2003 (http://politics.guardian.co.uk, accessed 24 March).

Guardian, The (2003) 'ID cards to cut asylum abuses', 23 May 2003, p 1.

Guardian, The (2003c) 'In brief', *epublic* supplement, 10 December, p 2.

Hall, S. (2000) 'Multicultural citizens, monocultural citizenship?', in N. Pearce and J. Hallgarten (eds) *Tomorrow's citizens?*, London: Institute of Public Policy Research, pp 43-51.

Hammer, M. (1990) 'Re-engineering work: don't automate, obliterate', *Harvard Business Review*, July-August.

Hampson, S. (2000) 'Location, location, location: the significance of place in the digital world', 1999/2000 lectures, London: Royal Society of Arts.

Handy, C. (1993) *Understanding organisations*, London: Penguin.

Handy, C. (1996) 'Beyond certainty: the changing world of organisations', in W. Dutton (ed) (2001) *Society on the line: Information politics in the digital age*, Oxford: Oxford University Press, p 114.

Hardy, W. (2003) 'The rhetoric of revolution', *E-Government Bulletin*, issue 136, 2 May (www.headstar.com/egb/).

Harlow, E. (2003) 'Information and communication technologies in the welfare services: wired wonderland or hypertext hell', in E. Harlow and S. Webb (eds) *Information and communication technologies in the welfare services*, London: Jessica Kingsley, pp 7-26.

Harris, J. (1999) 'State social work and social citizenship in Britain: from clientism to consumerism', *British Journal of Social Work*, vol 29, pp 915-37.

Harris, P. (2003) 'Parents can spy on kids' internet activity', *Observer*, 2 February, p 7.

Harrison, S. (1995) *Public relations: An introduction*, London: International Thompson Business Press.

Harvey, A. (2002) 'Content is key', *The Parliamentary Monitor – IT Briefing*, September/October, p 9.

Hastings, C. (1996) *The new organization*, London: McGraw-Hill.

Hawes, T. (2003) 'Implementing the e-organisation', Paper delivered to 15th Annual Conference of the Society of Public Information Networks (SPIN) on Electronic Public Information 2003, Birmingham, 22 May.

Headstar (2003) *Electronic safety nets*, London: Headstar.

Heckscher, C. (1994) 'Defining the post-bureaucratic type', in C. Heckscher and A. Donnellon (eds) *The post-bureaucratic organisation*, Thousand Oaks, CA: Sage Publications.

Heeks, R. (ed) (1999) *Reinventing government in the information age*, London: Routledge.

Heeks, R. and Davies, A. (1999) 'Different approaches to information age reform', in R. Heeks (ed) *Reinventing government in the information age*, London: Routledge, pp 22-48.

Hehir, J. (2001) 'Think about IT', *Local Government Chronicle and E-gov.uk, Special Supplement on Electronic Government*, May.

Hellawell, S. (2001) *Beyond access: ICT and social exclusion*, London: Fabian Society.

Henman, P. and Adler, M. (2003) 'Information technology and the governance of social security', *Critical Social Policy*, vol 23, no 2, pp 139-64.

Hennessy, P. (1999) 'The British civil service', *The Stakeholder*, Supplement, vol 3, no 3, pp 1-4.

Henwood, F. (2001) 'The ESRC innovative health technologies programme', *Social Sciences*, May.

Hill, A. (2003) 'Paedophiles set picture phone trap', *Observer*, 29 June, p 11.

Hill, S. (2003) 'System error: why UK Online failed', *Independent Review*, 30 April, p 11.

Hirst, C. (2003) 'The fallen grand "e" and why UK Online needs reinventing', *Independent on Sunday*, Business section, 13 April, p 6.

HM Government (2002) *In the service of democracy: A consultation paper on a policy for electronic democracy*, London: Cabinet Office.

HM Treasury (2002) *SR2002: a settlement for children and young people*, London: HM Treasury.

Home Office (2003) 'New drive to protect children online', Press Release 001/2003, London: Home Office, 6 January.

Hopkins, G. (1998) *Plain English for social services*, Lyme Regis: Russell House Publishing Ltd.

Horrocks, C. and Jevtic, Z. (1999) *Introducing Baudrillard*, Duckworth, Cambridge: Icon Books.

Hotopp, U. (2002) 'Teleworking in the UK' (www.nationalstatistics.gov.uk, accessed 9 November 2003).

Hudson, J. (2003) 'E-galitarianism: the information society and New Labour's repositioning of welfare', *Critical Social Policy*, vol 23, no 2, pp 268-90.

Hudson, P. (1998) 'The voluntary sector, the state, and citizenship in the United Kingdom', *Social Service Review*, December, pp 452-65.

Hughes, K., Bellis, M. and Tocque, K. (2002) *Public health and information and communications technologies*, Liverpool: North West Public Health Observatory.

HumanITy (2003) 'ICT, infrastructure and the delivery of services', Briefing paper no 5 (www.humanity.org.uk/articles/pub_infrastructure.shtml, accessed 30 May).

Huntington, A. and Sapey, B. (2003) 'Real record, virtual clients', in E. Harlow and S. Webb (eds) *Information and communication technologies in the welfare services*, London: Jessica Kingsley, pp 67-81.

Internet Intelligence Bulletin (1999a) 'Cybercafes and telecottages', 12 July.

Internet Intelligence Bulletin (1999b) (untitled), 8 August.

Islam, F. (2003) 'Workhorse with high aspirations', *The Observer*, 18 May, Business, p 7.

IT for All (2000), cited in DfEE (2000) *ICT: Preparing your application* London: DfEE.

Ivers, V. (1998) 'Advocacy', in Y. Craig (ed) *Advocacy, counselling and mediation in casework*, London: Jessica Kingsley, pp 25-34.

Jenkins, P. (2001) 'Healthcare to the home: the story of NHS Direct', Paper presented at *eHealth: a futurescope – Proceedings of the 3rd International conference on advances in the delivery of healthcare*, 4-6 April, City University, London.

Jervis, P. (2002) 'How technology is changing the world we're in', *RSA Journal*, December (www.theRSA.org/keytrends).

Johnson, C., Levenkron, J., Suchman, A. and Manchester, R. (1988) 'Does physician uncertainty affect patient satisfaction', *Journal of General International Medicine*, vol 3, pp 144-9.

Jordan, B. (1987) 'Counselling, advocacy and negotiation', *British Journal of Social Work*, vol 17, no 2, pp 135-46.

Jordan, T. and Taylor, P. (2001) 'A sociology of hackers', in A. Giddens (ed) *Sociology: Introductory readings*, London: Polity, pp 147-58.

Joyce, P. (2002) 'E-government, strategic change and organisational capacity', in E. Milner (ed) *Delivering the vision: Public services for the information society and the knowledge economy*, London and New York, NY: Routledge, pp 156-71.

Junnarkar, B. (2002) 'Sharing and building context', in D. Morley, M. Maybury and B. Thuraisingham (eds) *Knowledge management: Classic and contemporary works*, Cambridge, MA: MIT Press, pp 133-8.

Jupp, B. and Bentley, T. (2001) 'Surfing alone: e-commerce and social capital', in J. Wilsdon (ed) *Digital futures: Living in a dot-com world*, London: Earthscan/Forum for the Future, pp 97-114.

Kavanaugh, A. and Patterson, S. (2002) 'The impact of community computer networks on social capital and community involvement in Blacksburg', in B. Wellman and C. Haythornthwaite (eds) *The Internet in everyday life*, Oxford: Blackwell, pp 325-44.

Kearns, I. (2002) *Code Red: Progressive politics in the digital age*, London: Institute of Public Policy Research.

Kearns, I., Bend, J. and Stern, B. (2002) *E-participation in local government*, London: Institute of Public Policy Research.

Keep, G. (2002) 'Reaching parents: producing information that parents will use', *Family Today*, vol 4, pp 16-18.

Kendall, L. (2000) *The report of the policy forum on the future of health and health care in the UK*, London: Institute of Public Policy Research.

Kenyon, J. (2002) 'Technology budgeting basics: how much should you spend?', *lasa computanews*, issue 119/120, August, p 7.

Kerslake, A. (1996) 'Information management', in A. Kerslake and N. Gould (eds) *Information management in social services*, Aldershot: Avebury, pp 36-47.

Kevill, S. (2003) 'The BBC and E-Participation', *E-Government Bulletin*, issue 128, 10 January (www.headstar.com/egb/).

Kirkpatrick, G. (2002) 'The hacker ethic and the spirit of the information age', *Max Weber Studies*, vol 2, no 2, pp 163-85.

Knutt, E. (2003) 'It was never meant to be like this', *Housing Today*, 13 June, pp 20-1.

Korac-Kakabadse, A. and Korac-Kakabadse, N. (1999) 'Information technology's impact on the quality of democracy', in R. Heeks (ed) *Reinventing government in the information age*, London: Routledge, pp 211-28.

KPMG Management Consultants (1990) 'Runaway computer systems – a business issue for the 1990s', in Audit Commission (1994) *High risk/high potential: A management handbook on information technology in local government*, London: HMSO, p 57.

Krechowiecka, I. (2001) 'Out of harm's way', *Education Guardian*, 9 January.

Kreisky, T. (2000) 'Online government', *New Statesman Special Supplement: People Online*, 18 December, p xxii.

Kreps, D. (2003) 'Raising the stakes', *E-Access Bulletin*, issue 45, September (www.e-accessibility.com).

Kuhn, T. (1962) *The structure of scientific revolutions*, Chicago, IL: University of Chicago Press.

Laming, H. (1998) *Social Services Inspectorate: The chief inspector's annual report*, London: DoH.

Lasa Information Systems Team (2003) 'Working with IT volunteers', *lasa computanews,* vol 127, October, pp 4-5.

Lawrie, A. (1995) *Managing quality of service*, London: Directory of Social Change.

Leadbeater, C. (2000) *Living on thin air: The new economy*, London: Penguin.

Leadbeater, C. (2003) 'Amateurs: a 21st-century remake', *Royal Society of Arts Journal*, June, pp 22-5.

Leabeater, D. (1998) 'Government services in the information age: the consumer perspective', Paper delivered at a Fabian Society Conference on Reinventing Government, London, 10 February.

Leckie, D. and Pickersgill, D. (1999) *The 1998 Human Rights Act explained*, London: The Stationery Office.

Le Grand, J. (1993) *Quasi-markets*, Basingstoke: Macmillan.

Lenaghan, J. (1998) 'Introduction', in J. Lenaghan (ed) *Rethinking IT and health*, London: Institute of Public Policy Research, pp 1-15.

Lister, R. (1990) 'Women, economic dependency and citizenship', *Journal of Social Policy*, vol 19, pp 445-67.

Livingstone, S. (2001) *Online freedom and safety for children*, London: Institute for Public Policy Research/Citizens Online.

Local Government Management Board (1996) *Information for caring: GIS in social services*, Newhaven: LGMB.

Loga, C. (2003) 'Look out, baddies about', *The Guardian* (http:// education.guardian.co.uk, accessed 19 August).

LondonConnects (2001) *A draft e-government strategy for London*, London: Association of London Government/GLA.

Lord Chancellor's Department (2003) 'For your information: how can the public sector provide people with information on, and build confidence in, the way it handles their personal details?', Consultation Paper (www.lcd.gov.uk/consult/datasharing/datashare.htm).

Lovell, E. (2001) *Megan's law: Does it protect children?*, London: NSPCC.

Lowe, C. (2003) 'The secret of popularity', *E-Government Bulletin*, issue 137, 14 May (www.headstar.com/egb/).

MacArthur, B. (ed) (1993) *The Penguin book of twentieth-century speeches*, London: Penguin.

MacGillivray, A. and Boyle, D. (2001) 'Sink or surf?: social inclusion in the digital age', in J. Wilsdon (ed) *Digital futures: Living in a dot-com world*, London: Earthscan/Forum for the Future.

MacKenzie, D. (1999) 'The certainty trough', in W. Dutton (ed) *Society on the line: Information politics in the digital age*, Oxford: Oxford University Press, pp 43-6.

McCartney, I. (2000) 'Net gain for older surfers', *Housing Today*, 1 June, pp 16-17.

McLeod, M. (2003) 'Boost for groups to help bridge digital divide', *Voluntary Voice*, issue 175, June, p 11.

McLeod, J., Kosicki, G. and McLeod, D. (1994) 'The expanding boundaries of political communication effects', in J. Bryant and D. Zillman (eds) *Perspectives on media effects*, Hillside, NJ: Lawrence Erlbaum (in J. Blumer and S. Coleman [2001] *Realising democracy online: A civic commons in cyberspace*, Research publication No 1, London: Institute of Public Policy Research/Citizens Online), p 20.

McNevin, A. (nd) 'Hardware budgets cut as civil service revises IT expenditure', *Government Computing*, issue 8, 28 July.

McNutt, J. and Hick, S. (2002) 'Organising for social change: online and traditional community practice', in S. Hick and J. McNutt (eds) *Advocacy, activism and the Internet: Community organisation and social policy*, Chicago, IL: Lyceum, pp 73-9.

Mair, F. (2001) 'Telemedicine – a review of the evidence', in E. Carson, F. Harvey and M. Hughes (eds) *eHealth: a futurescope – Proceedings of the 3rd International conference on advances in the delivery of healthcare*, 4-6 April, City University London, London: City University, pp 13-14.

Maler, E. (2003) 'Shevaun case flags up web fears', *Third Sector*, 23 July.

Malin, N., Wilmot, S. and Manthorpe, J. (2002) *Key concepts and debates in health and social policy*, Maidenhead: Open University Press.

Mansfield, S. (1997) 'Content is king', *Information Age*, March/April, p 56.

Marshall, T. (1950) *Citizenship and social class*, Cambridge: Cambridge Unviersity Press.

Mason, P. (2000) 'The internet and beyond', *Community Care*, 19-25 October, p. 3.

Mathieson, N. (2003) 'Are councils meeting the online challenge?', *epublic: Guardian Society*, 8 October.

Matthews, H., Beale, L., Picton, P. and Briggs, D. (2003) 'Modelling access with GIS in urban systems (MAGUS): capturing the experiences of wheelchair users', *Area*, vol 35, no 1, pp 34-45.

Mayor of London (2002) *The Londonwide Domestic Violence Forum annual report*, London: GLA.

Microsoft (2003) 'Ingolstadt hospital: regional hospital improves patient care with better information flow' (www.microsoft.com/windowsxp/tabletpc/evaluation/casestudies/, accessed 16 November).

Miliband, D. (1999) 'This is the modern world', *Fabian Review*, vol 111, no 4, pp 11-13.

Miller, D. (2000) 'Citizenship', in N. Pearce and J. Hallgarten (eds) *Tomorrow's citizens?*, London: Institute of Public Policy Research, pp 26-35.

Mills, C. Wright (1970) 'The sociological imagination', in A. Giddens (ed) (2001) *Sociology: Introductory readings*, London: Polity.

Milner, E. (2002) 'Delivering the vision: an introduction', in E. Milner (ed) *Delivering the vision: Public services for the information society and the knowledge economy*, London and New York, NY: Routledge, NY, pp 1-16.

Monmonier, M. (2002) *Spying with maps: Surveillance technology and the future of privacy*, Chicago, IL: University of Chicago Press.

Moorhead, J. (2003) 'Mothers are doing it for themselves', *The Guardian*, 26 March (www.guardian.co.uk, accessed 19 August).

Morris, N. (2003) 'ID cards may include details of race, religion and political views, watchdog warns', *Independent*, 14 February, p 1.

Mulgan, G. (1998) *Connexity: Responsibility, freedom, business and power in the new century*, London: Vintage.

Mumford, A. (2001) 'Marketing working mothers: contextualising earned income tax credits within feminist cultural theory', *Journal of Social Welfare and Family Law*, vol 23, no 4, pp 411-26.

Mundy, D., Kanjo, C. and Mtema, P. (1999) 'Meeting training needs for information age reform', in R. Heeks (ed) *Reinventing government in the information age*, London: Routledge, pp 271-89.

National Grid for Learning (1997) *Connecting the learning society*, London: DfEE.

National Housing Federation, The Housing Corporation and Robson Rhodes (2003) *Small but perfectly informed: Information management for small housing associations*, London: National Housing Federation.

National Statistics (2003) 'Internet access: individuals and households' (www.statistics.gov.uk/pdfdir/int0903.pdf, accessed 10 November).

National Working Party on Social Inclusion (1997) *The net result: Social inclusion in the information age*, London: IBM UK.

Naughton, J. (2002) 'E-Blairs e-answers not enough', *Observer*, 24 November.

Naughton, J. (2003a) 'Cyberspace censors fail to filter out legal battles', *Observer*, 9 March, p 8.

Naughton, J. (2003b) 'Late scores: Germany 1 Microsoft 0', *Observer*, 22 June, p 9.

NeLH (National Electronic Library for Health) (2003) 'Electronic library for social care: health and social care interface scoping study: report' (www.nelh.nhs.uk, accessed 21 November).

New Statesman (2000) 'Roundtable discussion: the digital divide', *Special Supplement: People Online*, 18 December, pp xvi–xxii.

NHS (2001) Untitled (www.nhsia.nhs.uk/nhsnet/pages/default.asp, accessed 3 March).

NHSIA (NHS Information Authority) (2003) 'New NHS email and directory service now live,' News, issue 12, March/April (www.nhsia.nhs.uk/def/pages/inform/informish12/default.asp).

Nielsen//NetRatings (2003) '13 million kids using the Internet across Europe', Press Release, 29 September.

No 10 Strategy Unit (2002) 'Electronic networks: challenges for the next decade' (www.strategy-unit.gov.uk/2002/electronic/report_menu.shtml, accessed 25 May 2003).

Noble, M. and Smith, T. (1994) '"Children in need": using geographic information systems to inform strategic planning for social service provision', *Children and Society*, vol 8, no 4, pp 360-76.

Nolan, R. (1987) 'Managing the crisis in data processing', *Harvard Business Review*, March–April, pp 115-26.

NSPCC (National Society for the Prevention of Cruelty to Children) (2000) 'The internet – questions of child safety', Unpublished parliamentary briefing paper.

NSPCC (2003) '90% of adults worried about the threat posed to children by paedophiles in internet chatrooms', Press Release, 21 January.

ODPM (Office of the Deputy Prime Minister) (2002) *www.localegov.gov.uk: The national strategy for local e-government*, London: ODPM.

Office of the e-Envoy (2002) 'Electronic service delivery – Spring 2002' (www.e-envoy.gov.uk, accessed 2 October).

Office of the e-Envoy (2003a) 'Monthly report – 6 October 2003' (www.e-envoy.gov.uk, accessed 13 October).

Office of the e-Envoy (2003b) 'New draft smart card framework published by office of the e-Envoy' (www.e-envoy.gov.uk, accessed 7 August).

Office of the E-Envoy (2003c) 'Drive to encourage new internet users unveiled', Press Release, 10 March (www.e-envoy.gov.uk, accessed 10 March).

Ofsted (Office for Standards in Education) (2001) *ICT in schools: The impact of government initiatives*, London: Ofsted.

Oftel (2001) 'Towards better telecoms for consumers – May 2000 progress report' (www.oftel.gov.uk/cmu/toward00.htm, accessed 4 March).

Oftel (2002) 'Customers' use of mobile telephony' (www.oftel.gov.uk/cmu/toward00.htm, accessed 14 April).

Oftel (2003) 'The consumers' use of internet: Oftel residential survey' (www.oftel.gov.uk/cmu/toward00.htm, accessed 13 April).

Parker, S. (2003) 'Cross culture', *The Guardian*, 30 April, *Guardian Society*, pp 2-3.

Parkinson, D. (2002) 'Surfing the community', *E-Government Bulletin*, issue 114, 17 May (www.headstar.com/egb/).

Parkinson, D. (2003a) 'Technology and the movable citizen', *E-Government Bulletin*, issue 138, 6 June (www.headstar.com/egb/).

Parkinson, D. (2003b) 'The politics of the future', *E-Government Bulletin*, issue 138, 6 June (www.headstar.com/egb/).

Parkinson, D. (2003c) 'Tuning up your Wi-Fi', *E-Government Bulletin*, issue 130, 7 February (www.headstar.com/egb/).

Parry, R. (2001) 'In revolutions people used to say "keep your powder dry". Now they say, "keep your cellphone charged"', *Independent*, 23 January, *Tuesday Review*, p 1.

Parsons, C. (2002) 'Access all areas', *Charity Times*, December, pp 46-7.

Pearce, R. and Rosen, R. (2000) *NHS Direct: Learning from the London experience*, London: King's Fund.

Percy-Smith, J. (1996) 'Introduction: assessing needs', in J. Percy-Smith (ed) *Needs assessment in public policy*, Buckingham: Open University Press, pp 3-9.

Perri 6 (2002) 'Giving consumers of British public services more choice: what can be learned from recent history?', *Journal of Social Policy*, vol 32, no 2, pp 239-70.

Phillips, A. (2000) 'Second class citizenship', in N. Pearce and J. Hallgarten (eds) *Tomorrow's citizens?*, London: Institute of Public Policy Research, pp 36-42.

Phipps, A. (2001) 'Who's on line, who's off?', *Connections*, Spring, pp 10-12.

Pierson, J. (2002) *Tackling social exclusion*, London: Routledge.

Plant, R. (1991) *Modern political thought*, Oxford: Blackwell.

Plant, R. (1992) 'Citizenship, rights and welfare', in A. Coote (ed) *The welfare of citizens*, London: Institute of Public Policy Research/Rivers Oram Press.

Pleace, N. and Quilgars, D. (2002) *housing.support.org.uk*, York: Joseph Rowntree Foundation.

Pleace, N. et al (2003) 'From self-service to virtual self-help', in E. Harlow and S. Webb (eds) *Information and communication technologies in the welfare services*, London: Jessica Kingsley, pp 183-97.

Politt, C. (1990) *Managerialism and the public services*, Oxford: Blackwell.

Politt, C., Harrison, S., Hunter, D. and Marnock, G. (1991) 'General management of the NHS', *Public Administration*, vol 69, Spring, pp 61-83.

Poluck, M. (2003a) 'Electronic overload?', *Future Health Bulletin*, issue 18, May (www.headstar.com/futurehealth).

Poluck, M. (2003b) 'Seeing it wrong?', *E-Access Bulletin*, issue 38, February (www.e-accessibility.com).

Porter, M. (1985) *Competitive advantage*, New York, NY: The Free Press.

Porter, M. (ed) (1998) *On competition*, Boston, MA: Harvard Business School Press.

Porter, M. and Millar, V. (1998) 'How information gives you competitive advantage', in M. Porter (ed) *On competition*, Boston, MA: Harvard Business School Press.

Powell, S. (2003) 'Searching for a better result', *London Bulletin*, issue 24, July/August, Association of London Government, p 15.

Prasad, R. (2003) 'Big push for all-areas access to web', *Guardian Society*, 7 May, p 4.

Prime Minister and Minister for the Cabinet Office (1999) *Modernising government*, Cm 4310, London: The Stationery Office.

Prime Minister and Minister for the Cabinet Office (2000) *UK Online annual report 2000*, London: Cabinet Office.

Pring, J. (2002) 'Pain response', *Guardian Society*, 1 May, p 128.

Prochaska, F. (2002) *Schools of citizenship: Charity and civic virtue*, London: Civitas.

Puckett, K. (2003) 'Live and let dial', *Housing Today*, 21 February, pp 26-8.

Putnam, R. (2003) *Bowling alone*, London: Simon & Schuster.

Puttnam, A. (2003) 'Gotcha! Number's up for criminals as hidden police cameras take to the road', *The Gazette*, Hemel Hempstead, Berkhamsted and the Langleys.

Raab, C., Bellamy, C., Taylor, J., Dutton, W. and Peltu, M. (1996) 'The information polity: eletronic democracy, privacy and surveillance', in W. Dutton (ed) *Information and communication technologies*, Oxford: Oxford University Press, p 270.

Regan, S. (2003) 'Technology and systems of referral taking in social services: from narrative to code', in E. Harlow and S. Webb (eds) *Information and communication technologies in the welfare services*, London: Jessica Kingsley, pp 83-110.

Report of the National Working Party on Social Inclusion (1997) *The net result: Social inclusion in the information age*, London: IBM UK Ltd.

Reynolds, F. (2003) 'Promoting financial exclusion', *Poverty (Journal of the Child Poverty Action Group)*, issue 114, Winter, pp 10-14.

Ringen, S. (1988) 'Direct and indirect measures of poverty', *Scandinavian Journal of Economics*, vol 17, pp 351-66.

Robertson, J. and Wier, K. (1998) 'Using geographical information systems to enhance community-based child welfare services', *Child Maltreatment*, vol 3, no 3, pp 224-34.

Ross, J. (2001) 'Child-abuse evaluations go high-tech', *St Petersburg Times*, 3 June (www.sptimes.com, accessed 12 June).

Royle, S. (1999) 'See through Betsie's eyes', *Guardian Society*, 18 August, pp 6-7.

Ryle, S. (2003) 'Feel free to work from home – or a park bench', *Observer 5-Page Special Report: The Mobile Office*, 18 May, pp 5-8.

Safer Internet (2003a) 'Safer Internet 2003-2004 the ONCE workshop – young people's use of chat rooms: implications for policy strategies', no 23, March.

Safer Internet (2003b) 'UK: 20,000 child porn images a week put on Internet', no 30, November (www.saferinternet.org/news/archive.asp).

Safer Internet (2003c) 'UK: paedophiles exploit online file-sharing', no 24, April (www.saferinternet.org/news/archive.asp).

Safer Internet (2003d) 'Safer Internet in public libraries', no 24, April (www.saferinternet.org/news/archive.asp).

Safer Internet (2003e) 'A look at the eSafe programme', *Newsletter for awareness raisers in the EU Safer Internet programme*, no 21, January (www.saferinternet.org/news/archive.asp).

Safer Internet (2003f) 'US: web porn filers block health data, study finds', *Newsletter for awareness raisers in the EU Safer Internet programme*, no 21, January (www.saferinternet.org/news/archive.asp).

Safer Internet (2003g) 'Council of Europe: Internet literacy handbook', no 26, June (www.saferinternet.org/news/archive.asp).

Salomon, M. (2001) 'E-Health: global technology', in E. Carson, F. Harvey and M. Hughes (eds) *eHealth: A futurescope – Proceedings of the 3rd International conference on advances in the delivery of healthcare*, 4-6 April, City University London, London: City University, pp 25-9.

Sanderson, I. (1996) 'Needs and public services', in J. Percy-Smith (ed) *Needs assessment in public policy*, Buckingham: Open University Press, pp 11-31.

Sarson, R. (2002) 'You can take a horse to water...', *The Parliamentary Monitor*, September, p 170.

Sassen, S. (2000) *Cities in a world economy*, London: Pine Forge Press.

Save the Children Denmark (2003) 'Chat – a part of children's everyday life' (www.saferinternet.org/downloads/chatrapporr-summary.pdf, accessed 6 June 2003).

Saxton, J. and Game, S. (2001) 'Virtual promise: are charities making the most of the internet revolution?', *Third Sector Magazine*, Supplement, 22 January.

Schofield, P. (2003) 'It doesn't add up', *Community Care,* 24-30 April, pp 32-3.

Secretary of State for Health and the Home Secretary (2003) *The Victoria Climbié inquiry: Report of an inquiry by Lord Laming*, London: The Stationery Office.

Sen, A. (1985) 'A sociological approach to the measurement of poverty', *Oxford Economic Papers*, vol 4.

Senge, P. (1990) *The fifth discipline – The art and practice of the learning organisation*, USA: Currency Books.

Senge, P. (2002) 'Reflection on a leader's new work: building learning organizations', in D. Morley, M. Maybury and B. Thuraisingham (eds) *Knowledge management: Classic and contemporary works*, Cambridge, MA: MIT Press.

Servon, L. (2002) *Bridging the digital divide: Technology, community, and public policy*, Oxford: Blackwell.

Silverstone, R. (1996) 'Future imperfect', in W. Dutton (ed) *Information and communication technologies: Visions and realities*, Oxford: Oxford University Press, pp 217-31.

Sinclair, R., Hearn, B. and Pugh, G. (1997) *Preventive work with families: The role of mainstream services*, London: National Children's Bureau.

Skocpol, T. (1996) 'Unravelling from above', *The American Prospect*, no 25, pp 20-5 (March-April) (www.epn.org/prospect).

Sky News (2003) 24 March (www.sky.com/skynews/article).

Slack, N., Chambers, S.., Harland, C., Harrison, A. and Johnston, R. (1995) *Operations management*, London: Pitman.

Slater, A. (2003) 'Safety net', *YoungMinds Magazine*, no 65, pp 24-5.

Smith, C. and Webster, W. (2002) 'Delivering public services through digital television', *Public Money and Management*, vol 22, no 4, pp 25-32.

Smythe, J. (2001) 'Social capital and community involvement', Paper for the Audit Commission Seminar on Performance Indicators for Community Involvement, London, 4 December.

Social Exclusion Unit (1998) *Bringing Britain together: A national strategy for neighbourhood renewal*, Cm 4045, London: The Stationery Office.

SOCITM (Society of Information Technology Managers) (2003) 'Better connected 2003' (www.socitm.gov.uk, accessed 8 May).

Spicker, P. (1995) *Social policy: themes and approaches*, Hemel Hempstead: Prentice Hall/Harvster Wheatsheaf.

SSI (Social Services Inspectorate) (1997) *Responding to familes in need*, London: DoH.

SSI (2001) *Quality on the way*, London: DoH.

Stahle, P. (2002) 'Knowledge management as a learning challenge', *LLinE (Lifelong Learning in Europe)*, vol 1, KVS Foundation/Finnish Adult Education Research Society, Helsinki, Finland, pp 10-17.

Standage, T. (1999) *The Victorian Internet: The remarkable sory of the telegraph and the nineteenth century's online pioneers*, US: Phoenix.

Strassmann, P.A. (1995) *The politics of information management: Policy guidelines*, Conneticut: Information Economics Press.

Sun, The (2003) Full-page advertisement for working families tax credit, 11 April.

Sunstein, C. (2002) *republic.com*, Woodstock, NJ: Princeton University Press.

Surender, R. and Fitzpatrick, R. (1999) 'Will doctors manage?', *Policy & Politics*, vol 27, no 4, pp 491-502.

Takeuchi, H. and Ikujiro, N. (1995) 'Theory of organizational knowledge creation', in D. Morley, M. Maybury and B. Thuraisingham (eds) *Knowledge management: Classic and contemporary works*, Cambridge, MA: MIT Press.

Tambini, D. (2000a) 'Internet for all is a winning strategy', *New Statesman Special Supplement: People Online*, 18 December, p vii.

Tambini, D. (2000b) *Universal Internet access: A realistic view*, London: Institute of Public Policy Research/Citizens Online

Ticher, P. and Powell, M. (2000) *Information management for voluntary and community organisations*, London: The Directory of Social Change.

Ticher, P., Maison, A. and Jones, M. (2002) 'Leading the way to ICT success' (www.lasaorg.uk).

Timms, P. (2003) 'Remote control', *Guardian Society*, 5 February, p 12.

Townsend, P. (1979) *Poverty in the United Kingdom*, London: Penguin.

Transport for London (2003) *Oyster is here*, London: TfL.

Treanor, J. (1999) 'Computer age widens deficit', *The Guardian*, 7 July.

Valios, N. (2002) 'Maximum discretion?', *Community Care*, 18-24 July, pp 32-3.

van Vark, C. (2003) 'Online communities', *Third Sector*, 9 April, pp 18-19.

Varah, C. (2003) 'How and why I started the Samaritans' (www.samaritans.org.uk, accessed 14 April).

Walker, A. (2003) 'Welfare rights – on the case', *lasa computanews*, April, issue 124, p 3.

Watson, D. (2002) 'A critical perspective on quality within the personal social services', *British Journal of Social Work*, vol 32, pp 877-91.

Watts, O. (2002) Presentation notes for NSPCC Bullying. Full Stop Conference, Leicester, 3 December.

Webb, S. (2003) 'Technologies of care', in E. Harlow and S. Webb (eds) *Information and communication technologies in the welfare services*, London: Jessica Kingsley, pp 223-38.

Webster, J. (1996) *Shaping women's work: Gender employment and information technology*, London: Longman.

Webster, J. (2001a) 'Today's second sex and tomorrow's first: women and work in the European information society', in K. Ducatel et al (eds) (2000) *The information society in Europe*, Oxford: Rowman & Littlefield, pp 119-40.

Webster, J. (2001b) 'Women's access to ICT-related work' in W. Dutton (ed) *Society on the line: Information politics in the digital age*, Oxford: Oxford University Press, pp 167-9.

———

Weinberg, J. (2001) 'The national electronic library for health', in E. Carson, F. Harvey and M. Hughes (eds) *eHealth: a futurescope – Proceedings of the 3rd International conference on advances in the delivery of healthcare*, 4-6 April, City University London, London: City University, pp 69-70.

Wellman, B. and Haythornthwaite, C. (eds) (2002) *The Internet in everyday life*, Oxford: Blackwell.

Whelan, R. (2001) *Helping the poor: Friendly visiting, dole charities and dole queues*, London: Civitas.

White, M. (1999) 'Chancellor unveils plan for computers for the poor', *The Guardian*, 28 October.

Williams, J. (2000) 'Throw out your filing cabinets!', *Community Care: IT Supplement*, 19-25 October, pp 6-7.

Williams, P. and Maj, S. (2001) 'Drowning or waving?: is the Internet the lifebuoy for Australian general practitioners drowning in a sea of reference material?', in E. Carson, F. Harvey and M. Hughes (eds) *eHealth: a futurescope – Proceedings of the 3rd International conference on advances in the delivery of healthcare*, 4-6 April, City University London, London: City University, pp 81-6.

Williams, R. (2002) 'Dimbleby Lecture', 19 December (www.timesonline.co.uk, accessed 20 December 2002).

Wilson, C. (2002) *Designing web usability: The practice of simplicity*, A review of Neilsen Jakob, 'New riders', *lasa computanews*, issue 121, October, p 8.

Wilson, D. and Rosenfield, R. (1990) *Managing organisations: Texts, readings and cases*, London: McGraw-Hill.

Wintour, P. (2000) 'Ministers move to woo over-50s', *The Guardian*, 26 April, p 10.

Wintour, P. (2003a) 'Turnout: big boost from postal voting', *The Guardian*, 3 May, p 20.

Wintour, P. (2003b) 'Queen's Speech to pave way for ID cards', *The Guardian*, 7 November, p 6.

Woolgar, S. (1999) 'Technology and social exclusion: keeping a level head', Paper presented at Conference on Social Exclusion Through Technology, Office of Science and Technology, DTI, 8 March, London.

Worrall, L. (1994) 'Incorporating GIS into information management in local government', *Local Government Policy Making*, vol 21, no 2, pp 15-23.

Wray, R. (2003) 'A new kind of phone sex', *The Guardian*, 16 June.

Wyatt, J. (2000) 'Four barriers to realising the information revolution in health care', in J. Lenaghan (ed) *Rethinking IT and health*, London: Institute of Public Policy Research, pp 100-21.

Young, K. and Wilkinson, A. (2003) 'Webcasting and its contribution to e-democracy', Paper delivered to 15th Annual Conference of the Society of Public Information Networks (SPIN) on Electronic Public Information, 22 May, Birmingham.

Young Scot Enterprise (nd) 'YoungScot.org: the national youth information portal for Scotland', Edinburgh: Young Scot Enterprise.

Glossary

Accessibility: how readable and easy to use printed or website information is. It can also refer to the physical availability of, or skills to use, a computer or other device for using the Internet. It may refer specifically to the ease with which people with disabilities, such as vision impairment, can access the information on a website.

Asynchronous: the ability of a medium of communication to work even if the recipient is not present. Thus, a telephone is not asynchronous; letters and **e-mails** are asynchronous.

Back-office and **front-office:** terms used to differentiate between those systems and processes that a client or customer will see, use or interact with (front office) and those the public will not see or interact with (back office).

Broadband: a wide range of technologies that allow high-speed access to the Internet. This is particularly needed to download large files (for example, music and photographs).

Call centre: linking of telephones to computer systems to allow caller details to be called up instantaneously by customer services staff.

Chat room: similarly to a **message board**, this creates a space into which users log in to a website and are then able to see a list of other people logged in at the same site, under the same subject, at the same time. Users can then type in a message, which, once sent, any of the users in the room can read and respond to.

CRM (client relationship management) software: allows whole-life information on individuals to be held rather than isolated episodes; CRM on a child might include health, education and other details.

Digital divide(s): a polarisation between individuals (and across different groups in the community) who have access to information and communication technologies and those who do not. It may be caused by a lack of **accessibility** of the website related, for example, to socio-economics, culture, language, gender, ethnicity or disability.

Digital camera/video: electronic format that allows film and picture content to be used across a range of channels.

Digital interactive television (DITV): digital television is a telecommunications innovation that offers higher sound and picture quality than analogue television. When combined with a telephone line it can provide **interactive** services including **e-mail**, text messaging, voting, home banking and interactive entertainment.

E-commerce: the provision of commercial products and services through new electronic services.

E-democracy: electoral participation via new electronic services, such as Short Message Service (SMS) or text messaging.

E-government: the provision and organisation of public services (at local, regional or national levels) through new electronic channels. More broadly, it describes the use of **ICT** in support of citizen-centred democratic processes.

E-health: the provision and management of healthcare through new electronic services.

E-learning: the provision and management of education through new electronic services.

Electronic service delivery (ESD): covers a range of **e-government** transactions, which may include channels of digital television, websites, mobile technology, over the telephone and using **smartcards**.

E-mail: electronic mail is a way of sending messages and files from one computer to another via the Internet.

Information intermediaries: professionals, volunteers or others who guide and mediate an individual's online access to information and services.

Information and communication technologies (ICT): an integrated approach to using information technology (hardware and software of the computer or other device) and its transmission across a series of **networks**.

Interactive: a situation whereby **ICT** allows not just one-way transmission of information but also two-way communication. This fulfils a requirement for **online** social welfare service transactions, such as applying for welfare benefits.

Internet service provider (ISP): the organisation that connects a computer (or other **ICT** device) to the Internet.

Linux: operating software that is 'open source', in other words the code is open to all for modification, use and distribution.

Message board: a method and forum by which individuals accessing a website can post messages to a publicly accessible, **online** notice board, in a process similar to **e-mail**.

Network: a mechanism allowing computers to 'talk to each other' and share common materials and resources.

Online: a computerised activity while connected to the Internet, such as downloading a document from a website.

Personal digital assistant (PDA): hand-held computer.

Portal: a website page or pages that draws together in one place information or services on either a wide range of subjects (for example, local and central government departments) or on a specialised topic (for example, diabetes), which should be easy to access and easy to use.

Scalability: features that allow incremental development of an **ICT** system.

Short Message Service (SMS): a name for texting via mobile phone or other **ICT** device.

Smartcards: plastic cards, similar to credit cards, that can contain a range of data and be programmed for different applications, such as being fed into a machine to pass through a train ticket barrier, or used in a school canteen to register for a prepaid meal.

Telemedicine: a number of ways by which patients and clinicians can be 'connected' for immediate or indirect treatment through **ICT**, including by video conferencing and the Internet.

Teleworking: the use of **ICT** to enable people to work away from a central workplace, for example, their home.

Weblog: a mechanism that allows content (text, image, sound) to be posted quickly on a website in chronological order and sorted by a range of means.

Index

Page numbers in italics refer to case studies, tables or illustrations.

widening electoral participation 140-3
e-learning 7, 38-9, 69
e-mail 63
  front-line staff access 41
  inappropriate use scenarios *42*
  NHSmail *27*
  versus verbal communication 7
Earl, M. 52-3, 59, 94, 96
The Economist 129, 131
education authorities, school admission
  ICT systems *78*
education and e-learning 7
  ICT in schools 8
  and the National Electronic Library
  for Health (NeLH) *119*
  role of teachers as intermediaries
  116-17
Edwards, C. et al 74, 96
Edwards, S. 134
effectiveness *see* evaluation;
  organisational effectiveness
Electoral Commission 142
electoral process
  and participation 141
  see also e-democracy
electronic fingerprints 146
electronic patient record 75
electronic service delivery (ESD), and
  confidentiality 26-7
electronic tagging 8
eLSC (web-based electronic library for
  social care) 120
employment trends 13-16, 111, 127-8
empowerment of users
  consumer model 21
  and patient/doctor consultations
  117-19
  and procedural rights 18
  role of ICT 20
  in service development decisions 22
encryption technologies
  NHS e-mail developments *27*
  NHS/social services information
  sharing *79*
  use by paedophiles 31
ESRI *83*
ethnicity and ICT access 115-16
EU integration, future trends in policy
  137
evaluation
  causes of ICT failures 107
  examples of ICT failures 91-2
  of multi-agency information
  management strategies 59

  as ongoing process 106
  quality assurance processes 66-9
  social networks and 'process'
  enhancements 23
Evans, P. and Wurster, T. 40
Every child matters (DfES) 27
explicit knowledge/information 36-7
eye scans 146

F

failures *see* evaluation
family support services, development of
  multi-agency information
  management strategies 54-9
filtering software 30-1
financing arrangements 103
  public sector investment 91-2
  see also costs of ICT
'First Contact' 55
Fitzpatrick, T. vii
Fletcher, T. 116
Foley, P. and Alfonso, X. 109, 112, 134
'four-way flow' information
  management model *58*
Fox, J. 119
Freedom of Information Act (2000) 28
Freemail 125-6
FreeNets 127-8, 143
funding for public sector ICT 91-2
  see also budget and finance
  arrangements; e-government policy
Future Health Bulletin 116, 127

G

Gann, B. 117
Gartner Group 38
gender
  and commodification 22
  ICT access 1, 5, 7-8, 112-13
geographic information systems (GIS)
  81-2
'Get Started' schemes 132
Giddens, A. 6, 9, 15
Gill, T. 117
Giller, H. 77
Greater London Authority 115, 121,
  124, 129, *130*, 135
Global Consulting UK Ltd 115-16
globalisation 15
  and campaigns 143-4
Goetz, T. 149
Gold, S. 85

Also available from The Policy Press

Promoting welfare?
Government information policy and social citizenship
Dr Penny Leonard

This book links notions of citizenship with government policy to inform service users about their rights. It explores the role of government in encouraging or deterring the claiming of welfare entitlements as a way of understanding changing political perspectives and attitudes towards citizens and their social rights.

Information for citizenship is aimed at all those who are concerned about poverty, social justice and citizenship including students and teachers of social policy, politics and public administration; politicians and policy makers; service users, practitioners and welfare rights groups.

Paperback £23.99 (US$39.95) ISBN 1 86134 487 2

Hardback £50.00 (US $75.00) ISBN 1 86134 488 0

234 x 156mm 176 pages October 2003

Social alarms to telecare
Older people's services in transition
Malcolm J. Fisk

Healthcare, social welfare and housing policy agendas, while emphasising the importance of supporting the independent living of older people at home, have generally failed to take account of the actual or potential role played by social alarms and telecare.

This book draws on research and practice throughout the developed world. It documents the emergence of these important technologies and considers their potential in the contexts of healthcare, social welfare and housing.

Paperback £25.00 (US$40.00) ISBN 1 86134 506 2

234 x 156mm 304 pages June 2003

To order further copies of this publication or any other Policy Press titles please contact:

In the UK and Europe:
Marston Book Services, PO Box 269 Abingdon,
Oxon, OX14 4YN, UK
Tel: +44 (0)1235 465500
Fax: +44 (0)1235 465556,
Email: direct.orders@marston.co.uk

In the USA and Canada:
ISBS, 920 NE 58th Street, Suite 300, Portland,
OR 97213-3786, USA
Tel: +1 800 944 6190 (toll free)
Fax: +1 503 280 8832,
Email: info@isbs.com

In Australia and New Zealand:
DA Information Services, 648 Whitehorse Road
Mitcham, Victoria 3132, Australia
Tel: +61 (3) 9210 7777
Fax: +61 (3) 9210 7788,
E-mail: service@dadirect.com.au

Further information about all of our titles can be found on our website:

www.policypress.org.uk